T0245021

# A VERY SHORT HISTORY OF THE
# ISRAEL–PALESTINE CONFLICT

ALSO BY ILAN PAPPE

*The Ethnic Cleansing of Palestine*

*The Biggest Prison on Earth: A History of Gaza
and the Occupied Territories*

*Lobbying for Zionism on Both Sides of the Atlantic*

# A Very Short History of the Israel–Palestine Conflict

ILAN PAPPE

ONEWORLD

A Oneworld Book

First published by Oneworld Publications Ltd in 2024

Copyright © Ilan Pappe, 2024

The moral right of Ilan Pappe to be identified as the
Author of this work has been asserted by him in accordance
with the Copyright, Designs and Patents Act 1988

All rights reserved
Copyright under Berne Convention
A CIP record for this title is available from the British Library

ISBN 978-0-86154-971-9
eISBN 978-0-86154-972-6

Typeset by Geethik Technologies
Printed in the United States of America

Oneworld Publications Ltd
10 Bloomsbury Street
London WC1B 3SR
England

Stay up to date with the latest books,
special offers, and exclusive content from
Oneworld with our newsletter

Sign up on our website
oneworld-publications.com

# CONTENTS

# INTRODUCTION

Since 7 October 2023, when Hamas stormed into Israel in Operation Al-Aqsa Flood, the world's eyes have been on a country in which there seems to be no agreement, not even on name. Israelis call this land *Eretz Israel*. Palestinians call it Palestine. On 7 October, roughly 1,200 Israelis – the majority of them civilians – lost their lives, and 240 were taken hostage, many of them yet to return home. Israel's retribution, Operation Swords of Iron, has killed over 30,000 Palestinians so far; roughly a third were children. What follows is a concise history of how this came to be, for those who are seeing the conflict unfold for the first time as well as for those who have been engaged in activism for peace and justice in the region for many years.

The conflict didn't start on 7 October. The UN secretary general Antonio Guterres, when condemning the horrors perpetrated by Hamas, reminded the world that Palestinians have been subjected to '56 years of suffocating occupation' following Israel's victory in the Six-Day War in 1967. But the roots go further back than that, even deeper into the past than the founding of the state of Israel in 1948. Its beginnings can be found in the late nineteenth century. The history, like everything else, has become disputed – obscured by powerful political interests and polarisation on both sides. But I am a historian, and to provide context is not the same as making excuses.

Starting from when the first Jewish settlers arrived in historical Palestine to our present day, I want to shed light on the major events, personalities and processes to explain why this conflict has become so intractable. I make no claims to being comprehensive: there is a vast literature spanning decades for those interested in delving deeper into the issue. But I believe anyone who stands against oppression and injustice can understand the fundamentals of what we now know as the Israel–Palestine conflict. This book is my attempt to make it legible.

# 1

## WHEN AND WHERE DID THE
## CONFLICT BEGIN?

The short answer is in the late nineteenth century, back when Palestine was once more under Ottoman rule, as it had been since 1516, excepting some brief interregnums. It is estimated that by the end of the nineteenth century, around half a million people lived there, within three districts of the Ottoman Empire: Nablus, Acre and Jerusalem. The three districts stretched more or less over the area that today is Israel and the occupied territories. About 70% of the people were Muslims, while there were sizeable Christian and Jewish minorities.

Travellers and diplomats around the world marked the land on their maps as Palestine, and described its people as the Arabs of Palestine. Its inhabitants spoke in their own Arabic dialect, and had their own customs, including richly embroidered clothing, denoting village and tribal affiliation. But Palestine was changing, like the rest of the world, between the 1830s and the end of that century. The nineteenth century was the age of nationalism, and Palestine was not immune. Its urban elites, like those in

Damascus, Damietta or Beirut, revived their interest in Arabic literature and culture, forming a national identity from shared language. Intellectuals advocated for a new pan-Arab unification project, stretching from Morocco to Iraq and from Syria to Yemen and the Sudan. Nascent pan-Arab sentiment gained popularity after the rise of the Young Ottomans, a reform movement that sought to impose a Turkish national identity upon the entire empire – two-thirds of which was Arab. The 1876 Ottoman Constitution, a victory for the Young Ottomans, declared Turkish to be the only official state language. Arab subjects, including Palestinians, rightly bristled at this attempt at cultural colonisation. These trends would only intensify when the Young Ottomans' ideological successors, the Young Turks, took power in 1908.

The birth of a modern Palestinian identity coincided with a vibrant cultural renaissance, with pioneering writers, poets and journalists taking the lead, such as Ruhi al-Khalidi and Najib Nassar, to mention but two of them. In those days, it used to be said that the good books were written in Cairo, printed in Beirut and read in Jaffa. Palestine has never been separate from the Arab world; it is an integral part of it. It has also clearly never been 'a land without a people' as Zionists took to saying – ripe for the taking.

Alongside this cultural transformation, the Ottoman Empire, in its dying days, modernised the country. In Jerusalem and Nablus, new local governments were established, with reformist administrations. In the early twentieth century, plans were proposed and agreements were signed to build tram lines, provide electric lighting and repair old sewage systems. Provincial towns, in this vision, would become modern cities. However, the outbreak of the First World War meant that many of these grand ambitions remained on paper only.

At the same time as Palestine stood on the cusp of a new era, Zionism appeared in Palestine.

Zionism came as a foreign import. In the sixteenth century, it got its start as an evangelical Christian project in Europe. A significant number of Protestant Christians believed that the return of Jewish people to 'Zion' would fulfil God's promises to the Jews in the Old Testament. This would be a harbinger of the Second Coming of Christ, marking the beginning of the end of the world – a process many evangelicals wanted to speed up.

They were the first to regard the Jews as members of a nation or a race, instead of practising believers of a faith. They were particularly active in the USA and Britain and some of them sat in high office, people such as William Blackstone in the USA and Lord Shaftesbury in Britain.

What motivated them? Certainly not any sympathy for Jewish people. Some were outright antisemites, seeing Palestine as a dumping ground for Jews in the US, Britain and Europe, as they never accepted them as equal members of their respective nations. But it was also politically convenient, especially for those who were part of the governing elites. Jews, in their eyes, could be mobilised on religious grounds, to take the 'Holy Land', as they described Palestine, from the hands of the 'Muslims', i.e. the Ottoman Empire, which had been frustrating European imperialist designs in that region.

Jewish intellectuals and activists took some inspiration from this movement, regardless of the cynicism of its motives. The Christian fundamentalists of today, referred to as Christian Zionists in the USA, still subscribe to these ideas and are the most important pro-Israeli lobby in the USA, not only offering support to Israel but going further: backing Israel's annexation and Judaisation of the occupied West Bank.

However, we should be careful to differentiate Christian Zionism from Jewish Zionism. Jewish Zionism was driven by two impulses. It was firstly a response to the rise of violent antisemitism in Eastern and Central Europe, up to and including pogroms costing hundreds of lives. Europe has always had a problem with antisemitism – for centuries Christians condemned Jews as the killers of Christ, and added on various atrocities on top, such as the infamous blood libel. By the late nineteenth century, the fervour of modern nationalism led to the portrayal of Jews as a separate nation within a nation – intolerable and not to be trusted. But Zionism was not the instinctive answer to surging antisemitism at the time; in fact it was not even popular at first. Suggesting a group who have spent centuries in Europe transplant themselves en masse to a hot, dry land several thousand miles away with a language they don't speak is quite a hard sell. Thousands of Jewish workers organised themselves into socialist movements, believing revolution and the overthrow of the capitalist system would put an end to their oppression as Jews. Other Jews, undoubtedly thinking of the arbitrary brutality of the Tsar of the Russian Empire, held the view that building strong liberal democracies would offer opportunities for Jews to become full and equal citizens, thereby solving the 'Jewish Question'. The Holocaust shattered faith in these visions. After the death of over six million Jews, and years where concentration camp survivors languished in 'displaced persons' camps, with no European country willing to take them in, safety in formerly Nazi-occupied Europe no longer seemed possible. Only then did Zionism as a movement win genuine widespread support across the Jewish world.

The second impulse was nationalism. At the turn of the century, many groupings in Europe, under the yoke of large, unwieldy empires, like that of Russia and Austro-Hungary, began to organise themselves as national movements, fighting for the restoration of lost rights. And so there were demands for national-cultural autonomy from Poland, Ukraine, Czechia, Serbia and many more ethnolinguistic collectives. Jewish intellectuals saw the national framework as a means of modernising Jewish identity, to bring it bang up to date, so to speak. It meant reviving the ancient Hebrew language and re-reading the religious texts of

Judaism as political ones, the most important of these being the Old Testament. Unlike Orthodox Jews, the secular Zionists, like evangelical Christians, began to interpret the Old Testament as a historical document that showed that Palestine belonged to the Jewish people. Orthodox Jews regarded the Old Testament as a religious and moral tract compelling them to obey God's laws for humanity.

After a particularly vicious wave of pogroms in 1881 across the south-west of the Russian Empire, a group of young Jews made plans to settle in Palestine, hoping their zeal and purpose would inspire others to follow their example. They arrived in Palestine in 1882. They were able to buy land in Palestine with money provided by Jewish philanthropists and businessmen such as the Rothschilds. The land they bought was mostly owned by absentee landlords – that is, rich people who lived outside of Palestine, who had purchased land from the Ottoman state after reforms in Ottoman land law in the mid-nineteenth century.

Before these reforms, individuals generally couldn't own land as private property in the Ottoman Empire. It was leased by the Empire to landlords or farmers who built their villages on it. Many of these villages had been there for centuries. In Palestine some of these villages even predated the existence of the Empire. But under the new land regime, the villages' land, previously leased from the state, was now the private property of a landlord. However, in the Ottoman understanding, the fact of land changing hands didn't alter anything in practical terms. The land, it was understood, came with the tenants attached, i.e. the villagers and their villages. As the first Zionist settlers wanted to form their own agricultural collectives, their initial purchases were of uncultivated land, where largely no one lived.

This would change when British rule commenced after the collapse of the Ottoman Empire at the end of the First World War, as we will see later. The Zionist movement appealed to the British rulers of Mandatory Palestine to disregard the Ottoman custom. They demanded that the British recognise that land ownership meant they had the right to evict Palestinian villagers.

The first Zionist settlers, landing in Jaffa in the summer of 1882, had no idea about farming. They were mostly former university students, brought up in East European towns, with no instinct for agriculture. They needed the assistance of Palestinian farmers, who taught them how to till and plough the land, to make it bear fruit. Even then, the leader of that first group, Israel Belkind, never adjusted to farming work and spent his life as an itinerant teacher. These Palestinian farmers no doubt thought they were saving clueless young idealists from almost certain starvation, and probably had no inkling of how the Zionist project perceived them. But even in early Zionist propaganda, Palestinians were portrayed as aliens in their own native land at best, and at worst, as the appropriators of land that had rightfully belonged to Jewish people since the time of the Old Testament. Even at this stage, Zionist thinkers did not simply see the movement towards Palestine as a desperate escape from antisemitism in Europe. They saw it as laying the groundwork for taking over Palestine.

By the end of Ottoman rule in 1918, Jewish settlers were about 5 to 6% of the population. They were still a minority, but an organised one.

Concurrent with developments in Palestine, Zionists in Europe began to propagandise for a Jewish homeland in the corridors of power, essentially doing government diplomacy. These efforts were spearheaded by Theodor Herzl, an Austrian Jew, a journalist and a playwright, who has gone down in history as one of the founding fathers and driving forces of the modern Zionist project. He sought to consolidate a clearer political structure as a means to achieve Zionist aims. For that purpose, he convened the First Zionist Congress in Basel in 1897, which adopted a programme of establishing 'a home in Palestine for the Jewish people'. The programme made no mention of what would happen to the Palestinians if such a home was built. However, Herzl clearly wasn't optimistic about peaceful co-existence. In his diaries in 1895, he expressed hope that the 'penniless population', i.e. poor Palestinians, ought to be 'spirited away' over the borders to neighbouring countries.

Herzl anticipated that the Ottoman Empire, under pressure from European powers, would be willing to give Palestine to the Zionist movement. He even offered money – which he did not really have – to the Ottoman government in return for such an arrangement. But the Ottomans refused. The dream receding before his eyes, Herzl changed tack and suggested to the British government that the Jewish state didn't have to be in Palestine; it could be in Uganda, then controlled by the British. The British government was open to negotiation on this, but when Herzl presented it at the 1903 Zionist Congress it nearly prompted a split in the movement. Herzl's health was failing by this point, and he passed away in 1904. He is buried in what is now Israel, resting forever in a land he only visited once in his life. In 1905, the Zionist Congress definitively rejected the Uganda scheme. From now on, the Jewish homeland would be in Palestine or nowhere.

Other leading Zionist ideologues, such as David Ben-Gurion and Menachem Ussishkin, had little concern for governmental approval, whether of the British or the Ottomans. In their diaries, it becomes apparent that even in the first phase of Zionist colonisation of Palestine (1882–1918), they were already imagining a Palestine without the Palestinians, and openly discussed how that could be achieved. Unlike Herzl, who felt no particular affection for Palestine as a place, they also settled in Palestine themselves. The international legitimacy so vigorously pursued by Herzl did not matter so much to them. For them, the priority was establishing facts on the ground. Everything else would follow from that.

Chaim Weizmann succeeded Herzl as the leader of the official Zionist movement. He was a Russian émigré to Manchester, England. When he took over the leadership of the movement, he understood that his role was to build a strong pro-Zionist lobby both in Britain and in the USA. A lobby was needed because no matter how many times propagandists insisted Palestine was empty, it evidently wasn't. He needed to build a lobbying force that could persuade Britain to disregard the aspirations of native Palestinians and assist in establishing a Jewish state there. This would be sold to the British as a bulwark against the Ottoman Empire, a European outpost in the Middle East.

The outbreak of the First World War made this task a lot more difficult. Britain's main ally in the Arab world was the Hashemite dynasty. The Hashemites ruled the two holiest places in Islam: Mecca and Medina. In 1916, they were persuaded to revolt against the Ottoman Empire, then fighting alongside Germany and the Austro-Hungarian Empire on the promise by Britain that the Arab territories under Ottoman rule would be given to them as representatives of the pan-Arab national movement. These territories included Palestine.

If Britain had intended to be true to its word, the modern history of the Middle East would be entirely different. But during the First World War, Weizmann began to build connections between the Zionist movement and the British government. He correctly assessed that Britain was critical for the future of Palestine. Britain was already looking ahead to the end of the war and the presumed demise of the Ottoman Empire, carving up a new map of the Middle East. Palestine would play a vital part in protecting British imperial interests in the region.

Weizmann built a pro-Zionist lobby in Britain, made up of pious Christians who believed in the 'return of the Jews' to Palestine as fulfilment of God's will, antisemites who wanted Jews out of Britain, and Anglo-Jewish aristocrats, who would have been loath to immigrate to Palestine themselves, but saw it as a suitable destination for working-class East European Jews, whom they thought of as being communist troublemakers. In other words, the only thing these people had in common was wanting to establish a Jewish state.

It took two years – between 1915 and 1917 – for the Zionist lobby to persuade the British government that a Jewish Palestine would be a strategic asset for the Empire. What tipped the scales for Britain was the realisation that Palestine could be critical in defending the Suez Canal in Egypt. A friendly governmental regime there was hence vital. So the imperialists wanted Palestine for strategic reasons, Christian evangelicals wanted it to help bring about the end times, and the Jewish leadership wanted it as a safe haven for the Jews of Russia, as well as a means of forcefully modernising Judaism. To survive the new epoch, they thought, Jewishness had to be a nationality, not a religion.

On 2 November 1917, the British government made the Balfour Declaration, promising to make Palestine a 'national home for the Jewish people', while protecting the civil and religious rights of 'existing non-Jewish communities' in Palestine, i.e. the indigenous majority. This declaration was in fact a letter, penned by the British foreign secretary, Arthur Balfour, to the unofficial leader of the Anglo-Jewish community, Lord Rothschild. Arthur Balfour did not make this promise out of any concern for Jewish people's welfare. As prime minister in 1905, he in fact pushed for the 1905 Aliens Act, immigration restrictions designed to prevent East European Jews from arriving in Britain. Diverting Jews fleeing persecution to Palestine, a land he was equally unconcerned about, seemed to be the ideal solution.

Britain, alongside France and the US, emerged as the victor of the First World War. This alliance could now carve up the territories of the fallen Ottoman Empire as they pleased. To give this a veneer of international legitimacy, the victors founded the League of Nations, in principle an international organisation committed to maintaining peace across the world. Here the Mandatory system was devised, in which the League of Nations granted a member state a 'mandate' to govern a former colony, or an area that previously belonged to the defeated Empire. This was intended as a compromise between Britain and France, who saw their triumphs as a chance to expand their empires, and the US, whose president, Woodrow Wilson, had declared himself in favour of the other nationalities in the Ottoman Empire having 'an absolutely unmolested opportunity of

autonomous development'. In theory, the mandated territories of the former Ottoman Empire were only meant to
benefit from Allied administration until they could stand
alone, and they were recognised as on their way to full
independence. Iraq, for instance, became independent by
1932, Lebanon followed in 1943, and Syria was granted
independence in 1946. Only Palestine was the odd one
out – a direct consequence of Britain's old promise in the
Balfour Declaration.

By the end of 1918, Britain had completed its occupation of historical Palestine, what we now know as Israel,
the West Bank and the Gaza Strip. Palestine was now under
British military rule. In 1922, the League of Nations granted
Palestine official status as a British mandate, although
Britain had been de facto governing it as a mandate for
two years. The mandate agreed by the League echoed the
wording of the Balfour Declaration, directing the British
to 'secure the establishment of a Jewish national home' and
'facilitate Jewish immigration under suitable conditions'.

The British attempted to replicate the structure they
had applied in their other mandates. At the head of a mandatory country stood the high commissioner from the
mandatory power. There was then a government and parliament composed of the mandate's own inhabitants, with
some limited powers, but very closely supervised by the
advisers deployed by the European mandatory power.

But it was impossible for Britain to build this model
in Palestine. Britain got as far as appointing a high

commissioner, Herbert Samuel, but forming a government proved much more difficult – neither side was happy with the British proposals. The Palestinians rejected a legislative council that was tied to acceptance of the Balfour Declaration, and one in which they would always be outvoted. They also rejected all proposals for an 'Arab Agency', analogous to the Jewish Agency for managing immigration, as effectively treating them as a minority in their own country. And so, after agreement could not be reached, all powers, both executive and legislative, would be the realm of the high commissioner and his office.

At the start of the British Mandate, Jews constituted roughly 11% of the population. But they had been promised Palestine as their future home, by the League of Nations and in the constitution for Palestine drafted by the British. During the years of British rule, the British government tried to manufacture Palestinian consent to losing their own country by offering 'solutions' like partition, federation and forming a binational state. They did not offer to respect the mandatory principle that the majority of the people in a country have the right to decide its future, as happened in all the neighbouring Arab countries. And even when the Palestinian leadership was willing to countenance accepting the presence of Jewish settlers in a future Palestine, Britain did not dare to impose on the Zionist movement any solution that did not include a Jewish state over part or the whole of Palestine.

# 2

## THE QUIET YEARS, 1918–26

Palestinians did not intend for their country to be handed over, in whole or in part, to recent Jewish immigrants on the basis of diplomatic agreements they had no say in. Between 1918 and 1920, during British military rule, Palestinian thinkers and activists began to organise in Muslim–Christian Associations. These were formed to advocate for self-government and to oppose the implementation of the Balfour Declaration. By 1919, these organisations had grouped together under the banner of the Palestine Arab Congress.

The very existence of the Palestine Arab Congress dispels two myths often propagated by those who don't know any better: that the conflict is one between Muslims and Jews, and that Palestine had no national identity of its own before 1948. Since the beginning of the Palestinian national movement, Christians have played a crucial role in it. As early as 1911, two Orthodox Christian cousins launched the newspaper *Falastin*, championing an Arab Palestine and raising early alarm about Zionist ambitions.

This should give us pause for thought, as even today a common Israeli narrative insists that Palestine has no history of nationalism prior to Israel's founding. In 1972, the Israeli prime minister Golda Meir famously said: 'There is no such thing as the Palestinian people.' Too many Israelis still echo that sentiment today.

The years 1918–20 also saw the birth of a new Palestinian civil society, including political organisations, youth clubs and Arab newspapers. These groups also came together as part of the Palestine Arab Congress, functioning as the Palestinians' representative body. At the start of 1919, as the Paris Peace Conference was ongoing, this Congress convened and called for the renunciation of the Balfour Declaration. They saw Palestine as part of an independent Arab Syria. But as we can see, there was unity across religious lines against the attempt at carving out a new state.

The British responded to these developments by creating their own institutions. In December 1921, the high commissioner Herbert Samuel established the Supreme Muslim Council, which would have authority over Muslim courts and lands – the British were now trying to divide Palestinians according to religion. However, Muslims participating in this council remained highly political, and highly committed to the Palestinian cause. The grand mufti of Jerusalem, the highest Muslim religious authority in the country, Haj Muhammad Amin al-Husayni, was appointed head of this council – making him one of the most influential people in Palestine. He used his influence and authority to mobilise for nationalism behind the scenes.

Prior to the formalisation of the Mandate, Palestinians still hoped they could work with the British to ensure their future independence. But there were two events that put paid to that illusion.

In April 1920, a right-wing group of Zionists led by Ze'ev Jabotinsky marched through the Muslim quarter of Jerusalem's old city while Muslims celebrated the birth of the prophet Moses. Jabotinsky, who had been secretly arming Jewish men in 'self-defence' organisations, had predicted a pogrom in March and did his best to inflame tensions between Muslims and Jews.

In the run-up to April, the Hebrew press published articles campaigning for the building of a Third Jewish Temple on the Holy Mount, the site of the Second Temple, destroyed by the Romans in AD 70. This would mean demolishing the Haram al-Sharif compound, the third-holiest site in Islam, from where the prophet Muhammad is believed to have ascended into heaven. The rival religious claims to this site have yet to be settled in a satisfactory way for anyone, and could spark a wider conflagration involving much of the Muslim world at any time, if the Israeli government opts for a path of no compromise. A few years ago this may have seemed baseless fearmongering. But since November 2022, the Israeli government has included two political parties that are committed to building the Third Temple on the Holy Mount. The danger of an all-out conflict is now much closer than we'd like it to be. Back in 1920, these provocations led to street-fighting between young Arabs and young Jews, sharpening the divide between the resident population and recent Zionist arrivals.

Palestinians attempted to organise against implementing the Balfour Declaration using all the means at their disposal. Another wave of violence came in May 1921 in Jaffa, on the back of May Day demonstrations by ostensibly Marxist Jewish settlers who were supposed to be celebrating workers' unity. They had come from Tel Aviv, the settler-dominated city next door to Jaffa, and increasingly encroaching on it. As they marched through a Palestinian neighbourhood, the British fired warning shots to disperse them. Palestinians, fearing an imminent Jewish assault on their neighbourhood, began to attack the marchers, leading to a conflict that killed forty-seven Jews and forty-eight Palestinians. These two waves of violence, both set off by provocations and sustained by confusion, signalled that calm in Palestine could not endure in the face of an active colonisation attempt.

Nonetheless, up until 1929, there was relative peace in Mandatory Palestine; the tensions simmered but they did not reach boiling point. However, the calm was exploited by the Zionists to establish facts on the ground: to make their future state a fait accompli. This endeavour would have catastrophic consequences for the Palestinian people.

The British high commissioner facilitated Zionists building up the infrastructure for their future state, while Palestinian affairs remained in the hands of the British. The Mandatory authorities hence allowed the Jewish settlers to build their own educational system, their own industries and even military capacities, and all other services that one would think were the purview of the state. Simultaneously, Zionists like Eliezer Ben-Yehuda spearheaded the revival of the Hebrew language, at the expense of European Jewish languages like Yiddish and Ladino. A new Jewish ethnonational identity was being crafted in real time.

While the Jewish community was left to its own devices to effectively form its own proto-state, the Palestinian majority were treated as colonial subjects. The British administration imposed their own educational system upon the mainly rural Muslim population, and provided patchy state healthcare. State provision was vastly inferior to the infrastructure built up by Zionist organisations. Moreover, Britain did not allow the Palestinians to develop any real native governing elite, as they had in Iraq.

We can see just how differently the two communities were treated when we look at British policy towards higher education. The Mandatory administration enabled the Jewish community to maintain its pre-existing university, Technion, in Haifa, and to build the Hebrew University in Jerusalem in 1918 and open it in 1925. However, no resources were allocated for building universities for Palestinians.

In fact, during the Mandate period, there was only one government facility for training teachers in all of Palestine, the men's teacher training college, which would become the Arab College in Jerusalem. The British administration – with their previous experiences in India and Egypt – worried that an educated population would be too difficult to control. Palestinians nonetheless turned these institutions for teacher training into quasi-universities. In 1925, the Arab College could prepare its students to take the matriculation exam, to enable them to enrol in universities outside of Palestine. The College was highly selective and academically excellent. Many of its graduates pursued prestigious careers in neighbouring Arab countries and beyond. Had it not been for the catastrophe of 1948 – and the violent suppression of the vision for Palestinian statehood – these figures would have almost certainly been Palestine's future governing elite. Instead their talents were invested in countries like Iraq, Lebanon and further afield.

More significantly, the British administration tacitly tolerated the Zionist movement establishing its own paramilitary force, the Haganah. There was also evidence of co-operation between British security forces and the Zionist paramilitaries, a fact resented by Palestinians. Meanwhile Palestinians could not arm themselves or organise themselves on any significant scale.

But, as we've seen, the Zionist presence at this time was still relatively limited. And the impossible question – of how to build a 'Jewish homeland' in another people's country – had yet to be answered, and the British position remained subject to change. Especially in the first half of the 1920s, co-existence between the two communities remained possible. Even though Arab workers were excluded from the Zionist trade union Histadrut, there were still joint strikes by Arab and Jewish workers, such as in the tailoring and carpentry industries in Haifa in 1925. Arabs and Jews still founded new businesses together – more than one thousand joint businesses opened up in this decade. Facts were being established on the ground. But the catastrophe that followed wasn't inevitable. It only became so once the character of the Zionist movement fundamentally changed, as we will see now.

## 3

## WHY DID THE ZIONIST MOVEMENT BEGIN ETHNIC CLEANSING?

In the middle of the 1920s, the Zionist movement shifted from simply seeking to achieve a homeland where Jews would be safe, dependent on the mercy of greater imperial powers, to colonising Palestine in its own right, brazenly dispossessing the indigenous population. And moreover, it began to see this dispossession as *necessary* for obtaining that homeland. People do not often date the ethnic cleansing of Palestine to the mid-1920s, but what happened then laid the groundwork for everything that followed.

By 1926, the Zionist movement upturned many decades of convention in land ownership since the Ottoman reforms of the mid-nineteenth century. As we've seen, these reforms, meaning that land was no longer leased from the state, enabled the wealthy to become private landlords. In practice, individual farmers could not always show documents of tenure because they were registered collectively in the name of the village, which made it easier to evict them – peasants had little incentive to file claims with the government for their land. In this way, large swaths of land became owned by only a handful of landlords, many of whom were outside Palestine, now described as 'absentee landlords'. A few were Palestinian notables.

However, these reforms were never intended to change the day-to-day lives of the rural populations. When land was purchased, it came with the villages, and the villagers. Custom dictated that villagers had to fulfil certain obligations to the landlord – but there was never any question that the villagers were there to stay. That is, until the British administration changed the rules.

First, in 1920, the British administration removed many existing restrictions on land purchases, even if, conscious of Palestinian resistance, it placed some limits on Zionist purchases of land. But in practice it meant that the Zionist movement could buy as much as it could afford. It also reclassified Palestinian villagers, many of whom had been cultivating the same land for generations, as tenant farmers, and hence their presence became contingent on the landowner's will. Between 1921 and 1925, the American Zion Commonwealth bought 80,000 acres of land in what was then Marj ibn Amr (now the Jezreel Valley) from the Sursock family in Beirut. In 1929, the Jewish National Fund then purchased roughly 7,500 acres in what was then Wadi Hawarith, between Haifa and Tel Aviv, after the original Lebanese owner's heirs could not pay his debts.

In both these areas, the new Zionist settlers evicted, at times forcibly, the villagers and farmers who had cultivated the land. Driven by the ideal of Jews working on the land for themselves, Zionists sought, and were granted, eviction orders by the British authorities. And so the ethnic cleansing of Palestine began. It continues to this day.

The way Zionist settlements now expanded through the expulsion of local inhabitants indicates a change in the character of Zionism. What began as a movement to save Jews and modernise Judaism by transforming it into a national identity among others was now clearly a settler-colonial project, dependent on the subordination of another people.

Let me explain what I mean by settler colonialism. In classical colonialism, the colonies are ruled from the metropoles – as Britain ruled in India, or Portugal conducted itself in its African colonies. The aim is to turn the native population into loyal colonial subjects; the colonisers never aim to become the dominant majority population in the colony. In settler colonialism, the coloniser aims to wholly replace native society with the society of the coloniser. Settlers are frequently outcasts in their own metropoles – North America, after all, was colonised by people fleeing religious persecution in Europe. Settler colonialists are trying to build a home that wants them. And they are a useful way for imperial powers to expand their own spheres of influence – becoming friendly regimes in distant lands.

The trouble is that the lands are never empty. For settlers, desperate to impose their own culture and social system, the indigenous population, so obviously different to them, is an obstacle to be removed. This can never be done without brutality. In Australia, for instance, there were at least 270 massacres of the native population over 140 years of British settlement, on top of armed conflict and vast death tolls from epidemics. The process is not simply one of brute force, however. Settlers erase the history of native societies – dating it from when they themselves first arrived. Old customs vanish, and native food is appropriated as the settlers' own. Put simply, the land is not empty. And so the settlers empty it.

The late, great Australian scholar of settler colonialism Patrick Wolfe described the settler's attitude towards the native as 'the logic of elimination'. He argued that as long as elimination is not total, the settler-colonial project will endeavour to complete it. In other words, as long as Israel maintains a settler-colonial ethos, it will never peacefully co-exist with Palestinians.

These actions do not come out of nowhere. Before these acts of ethnic cleansing and genocide, and during them, settlers build an ideological justification; they create a consensus. They write about their intentions, sometimes directly and sometimes much more obliquely. We can see this in seemingly innocuous mediums like painting. Early Zionist painters depicted the landscape of their future home without any Palestinian villages in it. The villages marred the fantasy, and so they had to go. How did Zionists justify their attitude to the native population?

Like other settler colonialists, they depended on dehumanising the native population, who were portrayed as 'savages' or 'primitive'. A particularly potent trope in Palestine was that of 'nomads', people without any attachment to the land. This was in spite of many villages having existed for thousands of years. Simultaneously settlers claim to be driven by more noble purposes, i.e. bringing the benefits of modernisation (and civilisation) to a backward place. But settler colonialists differ from classical colonialists in a crucial respect here. Classical colonialists saw themselves as bringing modernity to the savages. Settler colonialists saw themselves as modernising the land, not the people. The people were inconveniences to be brushed aside for access to land. Even today, many Israelis repeat the myth that Palestine was essentially one vast desert until Zionists arrived and 'made the desert bloom'. No less a figure than Ursula von der Leyen, president of the European Commission, repeated this old cliché in her message to Israel congratulating it on its seventy-fifth anniversary. As we have seen, Palestine was in no way a desert, nor were its peoples nomadic, nor were they primitive.

While these illusions were propagated to make the Zionist project more palatable to Jews in Europe and beyond, Zionist thinkers knew full well that there was a native population that needed to be dealt with. Well before the 1920s we can find Zionist leaders deliberating about how the Palestinian population could be moved. Some of the Zionist ideologues hoped Palestinians would voluntarily emigrate to neighbouring Arab countries if provided with adequate financial compensation. But if not, forced transfer remained on the table. Zionist leaders and activists developed these lines of thought from the mid-1920s up until 1948, when the time came to put them into action. Now previously vague ideas were translated into a master plan that would result in the ethnic cleansing of half of Palestine's Arab population.

The massive land purchases in the 1920s, and the ethnic cleansing operations that came with them, helped bring an end to the quiet years. As the decade drew to a close, a far more fraught relationship between Jewish settlers and Palestinians would emerge, with violent clashes becoming more and more frequent in the 1930s. Both sides also clashed with the British authorities, who they saw as failing to protect them.

The signs of a disaster in the making were already evident as newly landless Palestinians, evicted from the farms they had made fruitful, were forced to move to the towns. These Palestinians were victims of nominally 'socialist' Zionist groups, known as Hebrew Labour, who believed Jews could only modernise themselves through engagement in productive labour. Hence they wanted agricultural work to become the preserve of Jews alone. Even Jewish employers of Palestinian rural labourers resisted this policy, as it amounted to letting experienced hands go in favour of settlers who may well have never worked on a real farm before. But landowners with this attitude were attacked and shamed publicly until they gave in. And so Palestinians, impoverished and dispossessed, sought work in towns.

In 1929, tensions would erupt catastrophically.

# 4

## THE EVENTS OF 1929

What happened in 1929 is known to the Palestinians as the Al-Buraq Revolution (*thawrat al-Buraq*). In Islam, Al-Buraq is a winged half-mule half-donkey, who carried Muhammad from Mecca to Jerusalem and from Jerusalem to heaven. Prophet Muhammad, in tradition, tied Al-Buraq to a crack in the Western Wall – enclosing the site of the Second Temple in Jewish tradition. Zionists, of course, call it a riot.

As in 1920, when Zionists marched through the Muslim quarter, the disturbance started in the old city in Jerusalem. Since autumn 1928, Zionists had been increasingly vocally challenging Muslim control over access to the Holy Mount or Haram al-Sharif. On 15 August 1929, the Haganah and Revisionist Zionists inspired by Jabotinsky staged demonstrations by the Wall, leading Muslims to mobilise for counterprotests the next day. Amid rumours and deliberate incitement, violent incidents between Muslims and Jews occurred throughout the week, culminating in seventeen Jews being killed after Muslims' Friday prayers on 23 August. This set off a chain reaction, and within one week, 133 Jews and 116 Palestinians lost their lives in the ensuing chaos. Violence did not stay confined to Jerusalem; it spread to other cities, most notoriously the Hebron massacre.

The Jews of Hebron were part of the small Jewish minority that existed in Palestine many centuries before the arrival of Zionism. They lived peacefully with the Muslim community. Both communities believe in the sanctity of Hebron, as it is the resting place of the prophet Abraham, revered in both religions. However, young Zionists, yeshiva students in modern European clothing, were unwelcome arrivals. As news from Jerusalem took hold, Muslims from villages just outside Hebron descended upon the town. Sixty-seven Jews were massacred, although some success-fully found shelter in the homes of sympathetic Muslim families. Now the Hebron massacre, a horrific atrocity, is weaponised by the official Israeli narrative to 'prove' co-existence isn't possible, and, ironically, to justify the subsequent massacres of Palestinians.

Although the immediate trigger for the events of 1929 was a religious one, the disturbances spread quickly and devastatingly as Palestinians witnessed the social order breaking down before their eyes. It was an outburst of frustration after a decade when the Zionist movement had moved in leaps and strides. In this decade, in the country-side, Palestinians could see what lay ahead for everyone: ethnic cleansing and purposeful immiseration.

As more and more Palestinians were forced out of agricultural work, shantytowns emerged. In the shanty-towns of Haifa, in the north of Palestine, a new form of Palestinian resistance took shape against Zionism and its British accomplices: guerrilla warfare.

Here a charismatic preacher came onto the stage, the imam Izz al-Din al-Qassam. You might recognise the name. The military wing of Hamas is named after him, as well as their early rockets. However, many secular Palestinian resistance groups also honour his legacy in introducing, in a doomed stand against the British, the methods of guerrilla warfare into the Palestinian struggle.

Al-Qassam was born in Syria in 1882. In 1919–20, he joined the revolt against the French occupiers, fighting them in the mountains. The French recognised he posed a threat and sentenced him to death. In late 1920, fleeing the French, he settled in Haifa. He preached in the Istiqlal Mosque, still standing today, and taught in a Muslim school. He quickly developed a name for himself.

Al-Qassam, with his background in anticolonial struggle, was able to enthuse young Muslims, living in the shantytowns around Haifa, to start their own paramilitary groups. They wanted to prepare for protracted struggle against British colonialism. However, faced with a large influx of Jewish immigration and increasing surveillance by British authorities, he was forced to show his hand prematurely. In the hills near Jenin, he and eleven others fought off a much larger British force for several hours in

33

November 1935, until al-Qassam and four others were dead. Haifa declared a general strike the very next day. You can still visit his tomb, near a Jewish town called Nesher – what was then Balad al-Sheikh.

His death inspired increasing numbers of young Palestinians to take up arms and to prepare to fight a war against Britain to force it to abandon its Zionist policies. He also established greater unity in the Palestinian political leadership, previously divided along family lines between the Husaynis and Nashashibis. Although al-Qassam's military revolt was destined to fail, he paved the way for the more organised resistance that would follow in the latter half of the 1930s.

# 5

## THE GREAT ARAB REVOLT, 1936-9

After 1929, the British recognised that what they were trying to address was a conflict between two peoples – both of whom they had made commitments to. They sent two commissions of inquiry to investigate the causes of the outbreak of violence in 1929. One was headed by Sir Walter Shaw and one by Sir John Hope Simpson. The Shaw Commission concluded that the violence was the result of the Zionist project of dispossessing the Palestinian farmers, and Palestinians' fundamental rejection of Zionism. The Hope Simpson Enquiry, which was carried out afterwards, reached similar conclusions. The final report recommended limiting Jewish immigration into Palestine.

Initially, the British government took the findings of these commissions very seriously and was prepared to change course. In October 1930, Lord Passfield (Sidney Webb) presented a White Paper that proposed restricting further land purchases and immigration on part of the Zionists, and was heavily critical of Zionist organisations for exacerbating Arab unemployment. This was a dramatic change in government policy. But even in 1930, there was a very influential pro-Zionist lobby in Britain. Under pressure from Chaim Weizmann, then leader of the World Zionist Organization, the British prime minister Ramsay MacDonald issued a letter as a 'clarification' of the White Paper in early 1931; in practice it was a retraction. Pro-Zionist policies would continue on the ground in Palestine, unimpeded.

The promise of a change that was swiftly withdrawn added fuel to the fire on the Palestinian side. They attempted to emulate the strategies of the Zionist lobby, but they were not anywhere near as well-resourced. Between 1930 and 1936, Palestinians attempted to alter British policy through petitions, demonstrations and conferences in London – all in vain.

In 1936, the Palestinian leadership knew something more potent was needed. An umbrella grouping of all Palestinian political organisations, the Arab Higher Committee, called for a six-month national strike in April 1936, demanding an end to Jewish immigration and land purchases and the establishment of a Palestinian national government. The younger and more rural elements of the Palestinian resistance did not stop at strike action. They staged an all-out revolt, targeting British and Jewish forces. It took three years for the uprising to be quashed.

Britain used brute force to suppress the revolt, including aerial bombardment by the Royal Air Force. Moreover, it deployed models of collective punishment now familiar to us all from the scenes unfolding in the occupied West Bank and Gaza Strip. Most shockingly, in June 1936, the British army blew up over two hundred buildings in Jaffa's old city, making over six thousand Palestinians homeless. Thousands of Palestinians were killed, many arrested and wounded. The military leaders judged to be behind the revolt were ruthlessly targeted, with a huge number killed. Beyond the leaders, large sections of the military elite, the most experienced forces on the Palestinian side, lost their lives. The goal was not simply to quash the revolt. It was to ensure that the Palestinians could not ever revolt effectively again. And indeed, in 1948, the Palestinians were swiftly overcome by the advancing Zionist forces intent on founding Israel.

Some months into the revolt, during a ceasefire, the British sent an inquiry commission, the Peel Commission, in search of a solution to the conflict. In July 1937, the commission recommended the partition of Palestine and offered more or less the creation of a small future Jewish state alongside Jordan (then known as Transjordan), which would annex what the report referred to as the 'Arab' parts of Palestine.

Places of particular religious and strategic importance would remain under provisional British rule through the mandate system until treaties were agreed between Britain and the two new states. As for the remaining Palestinian population in the land earmarked for the Jewish state, roughly a quarter of a million people, it proposed transferring them to Transjordan.

It is not surprising that the Arab Higher Committee rejected this recommendation entirely.

The Zionist movement on the ground was then under the leadership of David Ben-Gurion. He took a more conciliatory attitude to the British proposals.

Even though others in the Zionist movement demanded that he reject the recommendations, Ben-Gurion was willing to take the relatively small area offered to the Zionists as a state for two reasons. As he explained, the Jews were still a small community. Accepting the recommendations now didn't rule out taking more territory in the future. And secondly, it cost him nothing to extend an olive branch to the British in this way, because he knew with absolute certainty that the Palestinians would reject the proposals. He was already thinking ahead. With his closest confidantes and his son, he discussed the possibilities of Zionists preparing to transfer Palestinians from Jewish state territory; he intuited that the British would not aid in this.

Realising a solution on the ground was not forthcoming, Britain contemplated taking the Peel proposal to the League of Nations. Before it did that, it sent another inquiry commission to Palestine, the Woodhead Commission, in 1938. This commission rejected partition as recommended by the Peel Commission as completely impracticable, as any partition would require vast and forcible population transfer of the Palestinians. In the preferred solution of the Woodhead Commission, there would be a small Jewish state, a larger Palestinian state, and land in the north and south, as well as Jerusalem, would remain Mandate territory. These would all be joined in a customs union. This proposal was even controversial among the commission members. In short, the Woodhead Commission made clear that it was not possible, without huge injustice, for the bulk of Mandatory Palestine to become a Jewish state.

Following this realisation, it was easier to bring the revolt to an end, as Palestinian leaders hoped Britain finally understood it was impossible to impose a Jewish state on the Palestinians. The British government published a White Paper in May 1939 that more or less said as much. It declared that given there were now over 450,000 Jews settled in Palestine, Britain had fulfilled its obligation under the Balfour Declaration to provide a 'national home'. It recommended that Palestine become an independent state in ten years, to be governed jointly by Palestinians and Jews. Jewish immigration and land purchases would be limited for at least the next five years. Predictably, this made no one happy.

The Zionist leadership rejected the White Paper as a complete contradiction of the commitments made in the Balfour Declaration. The Palestinian Arab Higher Committee was disappointed that the White Paper still expressed affirmation of a 'Jewish national home' and only proposed limited Jewish immigration for five years. Only a few months after the White Paper, Hitler and Stalin invaded Poland: the Second World War had begun. Britain was conscious both of Hitler's attempts to win over newly independent states like Iraq and the need to place Allied troops in Palestine as a strategically critical staging post in the Middle East. And so, even as Jewish people across Nazi-occupied Europe sought refuge elsewhere, Britain kept the doors of Palestine firmly closed.

Hitler's brisk sweep through Europe and the consequent mass murder of Jewish people hardened Zionist attitudes. They no longer wanted to compromise with Palestinians in any way. At the Biltmore Hotel in New York in May 1942, the Zionist leadership declared its intention to turn all of historical Palestine into a Jewish state. The New York location is significant. The Zionist movement understood that the keys to Palestine's future might not be in Britain's hands for much longer, now that a new world power was entering the spotlight. The Zionist movement was keen to be as strong in the US as it was previously in Britain.

Palestinians had no equivalent to the Zionist lobby in Britain or the US in 1942. The Palestinian leadership had still not recovered from its utter decimation during the Arab Revolt. Most of its prominent politicians were exiled or in prison. The leading figure in Palestinian politics at that time was Haj Muhammad Amin al-Husayni, the grand mufti of Jerusalem, who had initially been supported by the British in the early 1920s.

By the 1930s, he had founded his own political organisation with members from his influential family as well as other local elites. Another Palestinian grouping was centred on another elite family, the Nashashibis. These and other groups were represented on the Arab Higher Committee, but Haj Amin remained the most high-profile figure and was chair of the Committee.

When the Arab Revolt broke out, the British administration declared that the Committee was illegal and relieved Haj Amin of his position as president of the Supreme Muslim Council. In July 1937, the British authorities issued a warrant for his arrest. Tipped off in advance, he managed to escape initially to Damascus, but landed in Nazi Germany in 1941, making radio broadcasts to mobilise Arab Muslims against the British. At the time of the Second World War, he was not alone in acting according to the maxim: the enemy of my enemy is my friend. His flirtation with the Nazis was short and insignificant, making no difference one way or the other to the war effort. However, his association with the Nazis is still used to discredit the Palestinian liberation movement in the Israeli narrative. Sometimes it gets taken to absurd levels, such as when the prime minister Benjamin Netanyahu claimed that it was Haj Amin who gave Hitler the idea for death camps, and that otherwise Hitler would have just deported the Jews.

With Haj Amin in exile, and the remainder of the Palestinian leadership mainly criminalised, the Zionist movement was free to agitate for a de-Arabised Palestine with Anglo-American blessing. The Palestinians simply did not have political clout comparable to that of the Zionists. Their only hope now was to rely on help from neighbouring Arab countries, but they themselves were not yet established as proper nation states.

After the Holocaust, where over six million Jews perished across Europe, European powers, eager to wash their own consciences clean, had even less sympathy for the Palestinians. This was not out of any particular concern for Jews – at least 250,000 Jews languished in Displaced Persons Camps in Central Europe long after the war had concluded. But the future of the Jewish people, in the eyes of Britain and the USA, had to be settled. Many survivors of the Holocaust no longer had any homes to go back to in Europe.

# 6

## ON THE ROAD TO THE NAKBA, 1945–7

The British Mandate would end in 1948. In the three years between the end of the war and British departure, we can identify three concurrent processes resulting in the catastrophe for the Palestinian people known as the Nakba, and the establishment of the state of Israel.

The first was the failure of diplomatic efforts to bring an end to the conflict between Palestinians and Zionist settlers. The second was the inadequacy of the Arab world's attempts to make a meaningful impact on the situation on the ground. The third was the final preparation on the Zionist side for the ethnic cleansing of Palestine – which would be translated into action as soon as the British left in 1948.

### THE DIPLOMATIC EFFORT, 1945–7

Shortly after the Second World War concluded, Britain still hoped to find a solution that both sides could live with. To that end, the British government enlisted the Americans, establishing a new Anglo-American Committee in November 1945, tasked with the last international effort to resolve the conflict before the end of the Mandate. The Committee arrived in Palestine in early 1946, and made its report in April of that year.

The report succeeded as a socio-economic investigation – providing meticulously detailed information about the demography, economy, education and politics of Mandatory Palestine. Scholars use it as a resource to this day. But in terms of finding a real solution, the report offered nothing both sides hadn't heard dozens of times before. It did not recommend a Jewish state, or an independent Palestinian state, but proposed an extended British presence in Mandatory Palestine, overseeing autonomous Arab and Jewish enclaves. Both sides rejected this idea out of hand, realising they were being denied the very democratic rights that the new international order was supposedly founded on.

By the beginning of 1947, Britain had had enough of Palestine. It was at last starting to dawn on the British that they could not obtain Palestinian consent for the promise they made to Jewish people in the Balfour Declaration, i.e. for a 'Jewish national home'. And moreover, what the Zionist movement now meant by a 'Jewish national home' was irreconcilable with extending national independence to Palestinians. The British postwar economy creaked under the weight of a bitter winter and the huge reconstruction effort needed to provide homes after the Blitz. Moreover, the Labour government under Clement Attlee had determined that the British Empire was now an expensive liability, and much of it just had to go. Meanwhile, the Second World War had radicalised the Zionist movement and they were no longer happy with letting Britain drag its feet. Militant Zionist groups perpetrated terrorist attacks to push the British along. In July 1946, the Zionist underground organisation Irgun had blown up the British Mandate's central offices at the King David Hotel in Jerusalem, killing ninety-one people. Zionist insurgents frequently targeted British soldiers for kidnapping and murder.

Seeing no end in sight, on 1 February 1947 Britain referred the future of Palestine to the UN. The UN was less than two years old at this point, and had no experience in addressing decades-long conflicts like the situation in Palestine.

Moreover, most of the colonised world was still not represented in the UN, as the main wave of decolonisation was yet to come. On most issues, the UN would wind up as a diplomatic battlefield between the two superpowers, the US and the USSR. However, anyone hoping for a showdown between two power blocs on Palestine would be disappointed. Both states absented themselves from participating in the committee for investigating the situation. In May 1947, the UN appointed two delegates each from eleven 'neutral' member states to find a solution to what it termed the 'Palestine Question'.

This was the UN Special Committee on Palestine (UNSCOP). It arrived in Palestine in June, and held many public hearings, before it submitted a final report recommending partition in September 1947. The Palestinian political leadership, represented by the Arab Higher Committee, boycotted the committee's processes. It demanded that Palestine be treated the same as all its neighbouring Arab countries, which had obtained full independence once their respective mandates had ended. The Palestinians refused to legitimise a process that considered their right to independence as up for negotiation. They compared their situation to that of Algeria and asked the UN whether the Algerians would agree to negotiate their right to their own country with French settlers in the future.

By this point, some of the more perceptive Palestinian politicians and intellectuals had cottoned on to what the Zionist leadership actually wanted: as much of Palestine as they could get with as few Palestinians as possible. They were frustrated that Zionism's own plans weren't discussed seriously as an obstacle to resolving the conflict in the halls of the UN. Ultimately diplomatic efforts failed because no one could provide any justification for why Palestine was being handled as an exceptional case – a place where the much-vaunted principles of 'equal rights and self-determination of peoples' in the UN charter did not apply.

## THE ARAB WORLD AND
## PALESTINE, 1945-7

The Arab world supported Palestine's rejection of UNSCOP, vocalising its solidarity through the position of the Arab League, a new organisation founded in 1945. Only one Arab state differed: Transjordan. This would affect the course of Palestinian history considerably. In order to understand why the Jordanians deviated from the consensus Arab position, we need to go back in time to the making of Jordan as a state.

Transjordan was established as a British protectorate in 1921; formerly, like Palestine, it was part of the Ottoman Empire. When Transjordan was occupied by the British in 1918, the initial plan was to incorporate it into Mandatory Palestine.

But then developments in Hejaz, the region containing Islam's holiest cities, Mecca and Medina, complicated the situation in Transjordan. During the First World War, a local dynasty, the Hashemites, declared the Hejaz as an independent kingdom under their rule. The British made an alliance with them: in return for the Hashemites fighting against the Ottomans, the British would recognise them as an independent state. Moreover, the British promised that the Hashemites would be able to establish new royal houses in what would become Syria and Iraq, to be headed by the heirs of Hussein bin Ali, who was the sharif of Mecca and the king of Hejaz.

But none of these promises were easy to keep. In the Arabian Peninsula the British had also supported the arch-rivals of the Hashemites, the House of Saud. So Britain did not intervene when the Saudis waged a war against the Hashemites, occupying Hejaz in 1924 and making it an integral part of Saudi Arabia.

Originally the British promised the kingdom of Iraq to Sharif Hussein's elder son, Abdullah, and the kingdom of Syria to his younger son, Faisal. But Britain had also agreed that Syria would be under France's control in the Sykes–Picot Agreement, so it was no longer theirs to give away. (Making contradictory promises to different parties is something of a theme in Britain's foreign relations.)

The two sons decided to take action themselves, and changed the map of the region. Faisal, with the help of the legendary Lawrence of Arabia, the British progenitor of the alliance between the British and the Hashemites, exploited the fact that until 1920 there were no French troops on the ground in the Eastern Mediterranean. He entered Damascus in 1918 as the new ruler, not only of the city but of what he called the Greater Syria, including Lebanon, Jordan, Syria, Israel and the Palestinian territories of today. He lasted a little under two years with no official international recognition; he was forced to surrender to the French in July 1920.

The British sought to appease him by installing him as king in Iraq in 1921 – leaving no throne for his elder brother Abdullah. In 1920, Abdullah had marched out of Hejaz with 20,000 men behind him, supposedly to 'liberate' Syria from the French. His troops were stationed in Amman, Transjordan.

While Abdullah was waiting there, threatening to occupy Syria, the British reshuffled the parts of the Arab world that were under their control at a conference in Cairo in May 1921. The conference was led by the then British secretary of state for the colonies, Winston Churchill. He proposed that Abdullah would be given Transjordan as his new kingdom. Transjordan became Jordan and was now its own state, separate from Mandatory Palestine.

The right wing of the Zionist movement, led by Ze'ev Jabotinsky, did not accept this loss of territory, seeing Transjordan as part of the future Jewish state. Even today, the lands in Jordan are shown as part of Israel on the flag of Beitar, a right-wing Zionist youth movement descended from Jabotinsky's organisation.

However, the Labour Zionists, who at the time dominated the Zionist movement as a whole, welcomed Hashemite control over Transjordan. From the beginning, Abdullah was in close contract with the Jewish Agency, effectively the Zionist administration for the Jewish community during the Mandatory period. He wanted to expand his kingdom, composed of relatively arid land, with an eye to the fertile territory in Mandatory Palestine. As well as the

Jewish Agency, he developed a working relationship with the pragmatic Nashashibi family in the Palestinian leadership, a more moderate faction than the Husaynis.

Let's return to 1947. By the time UNSCOP was formed and began its deliberations, the relationship between the Jewish Agency and Abdullah had reached a more practical stage. It seems that both sides agreed that Transjordan could expand into parts of Mandatory Palestine in return for its tacit consent for the establishment of a Jewish state in Palestine. This is why Abdullah was the only Arab leader willing to meet with UNSCOP.

The other members of the Arab League had no inkling of these secret agreements. The Arab League continued to try to pressure the UN into adopting an approach to Palestine based on the principles of democracy and self-determination. After the UN came out in favour of partition, the Arab League began building a volunteer army, the Arab Liberation Army, and was prepared to contemplate a military operation in Mandatory Palestine, should diplomatic efforts all fail.

## ZIONIST STRATEGIES, 1945–7

Unlike the Palestinians, who focused their efforts on securing international legitimacy, the Zionist movement saw the end of the Mandate as an opportunity to swiftly establish their dominance on the ground.

The Zionist movement had been demanding that the Mandate end since 1942. For them, the British couldn't leave a day too soon. Throughout 1945–7, they laid the groundwork to take over the entire country's administration.

The Palestinian leadership believed, with no small amount of naivety, that as they were both the native population and the majority, the UN would obviously make Palestine a state for the Palestinians. The Zionist leaders believed that actions speak louder than words. They correctly calculated that the international community would not help the Palestinians reclaim what the Zionists had taken by force to begin with. So they planned to conquer all key strategic posts as soon as British troops vacated them: radio, postal services, telecommunications, railways, air space, public transport, banking and, of course, land.

Over two years, they intensified the build–up of military forces, obtaining arms from abroad and devising a system of conscription for all young Jewish men and women in Palestine. The British considered the Haganah, which transformed from a paramilitary organisation into essentially the regular army of a state that did not yet exist, to be the second most powerful military force in the Middle East. Even survivors of the Holocaust in Europe, many of them still stuck in Displaced Persons Camps, were recruited into Zionist military organisations. The process of joining a Zionist army was much smoother than getting a visa to the US.

Towards the end of 1947, all eyes were on New York. The UN was, at long last, about to make a final decision about the future of Palestine. On 29 November, the UN General Assembly voted for Resolution 181, now infamous in international law. It declared itself in favour of the partition of Palestine. Zionists celebrated, as Israel still does today – they had finally got the Jewish state they had been promised. For Palestinians, it's the day the Nakba began, the day that fired a warning shot for a catastrophe that they still endure in our times.

# 7

# THE PARTITION RESOLUTION
# AND ITS AFTERMATH

Before we turn to the impact of the Partition Resolution on the ground, we need to examine the perplexing geo-political manoeuvring at the UN more closely. UNSCOP, the special committee made up of eleven member states, could not actually arrive at a consensus position on what was to be done in Palestine. It produced two proposals, one by the minority, and one by the majority.

The minority plan recommended a binational federal state in Palestine, divided into Arab and Jewish nations, with Jewish immigration permitted in the Jewish nation. The federal government would be elected by all adult citizens across the Arab and Jewish states. In UNSCOP, this was only supported by India, Iran and Yugoslavia. The majority supported the partition of Palestine into two states.

The majority proposal offered 56% of Palestine for a Jewish state, which included most of the important UN concessions such as electricity, ports and phosphates within that territory, and 43% for a Palestinian state. Jerusalem and its surroundings would be governed as a *corpus sep-aratum*, i.e. an international enclave. The Jewish state would be made up of almost equal numbers of Jews and Palestinians, and the Arab state would have a vast majority of Palestinians. Both communities could decide where to vote and where to belong to as citizens; the two states were supposed to have a common currency and economy and a jointly agreed immigration policy.

On 29 November 1947, the UN General Assembly voted only on the majority proposal, slightly amended after discussion by an Ad Hoc Committee of all member states. Ultimately thirty-three states voted in favour of par-tition, with thirteen votes against and ten abstentions. By the skin of their teeth, the Zionist movement had scraped a majority of two-thirds. It almost didn't happen.

Although the UN, then composed of fifty-seven nations, was still dominated by European imperial powers, the US and the USSR, there were member states that remem-bered only too well the brutality of colonisation, such as Liberia and Haiti. The vote was initially due to take place on 26 November, but the Zionist movement worried they wouldn't be able to secure the votes they needed. So, through some diplomatic wrangling, it was postponed until 29 November. The Zionist lobby in the US urged the US government to pressure recalcitrant states into voting for partition – a key milestone, as it entailed international recognition of a Jewish state. The US government, which was already pro-Zionist by default by this point, was only too happy to comply, and promised hesitant states funding for developing their countries, or threatening to withdraw such funding. This is the classic carrot-and-stick approach wealthier nations deploy in diplomacy.

Resolution 181 also proposed a timeline for the next year. It set the date for the termination of the British Mandate as 14 May 1948. Until then, Britain would still be responsible for law and order, assisted by a new UN Palestine Committee in implementing the partition plan.

Both the US and USSR, despite being rival powers, came together to support the partition plan. The USSR upturned decades of staunch anti-Zionism as part and parcel of Communism and came out in favour of the possibility of partition as early as May 1947. Even though Arab states were convinced the USSR would side with them, Stalin saw Zionism as a way of weakening Britain's influence in the region, and facilitated mass emigration of Jews from the USSR and Poland into the Displaced Persons Camps – the ultimate destination being Palestine.

In the US, an assertive Zionist lobbying effort strong-armed the American president into supporting partition, and convincing others to support it. This was despite the scepticism of the US State Department and its experts on the Middle East, who thought such an embrace of Zionism harmed other US interests in the region.

Meanwhile, the British government was hardly wild about the prospect of a Palestinian Arab state, which it disparagingly dubbed the 'Mufti state'. Since the Great Arab

Revolt in 1936, Mufti Haj Amin al-Husayni had been the arch-enemy of Britain in the Arab world. Even though he and many other Palestinian leaders who fled after the revolt were not permitted to return to Palestine, he still seemed to be leading the Palestinian national movement from his exile in Cairo. The British believed he would become the leader of the future Palestinian state and act against their interests in the region.

In order to avert this prospect, Britain opted to strengthen the position of King Abdullah of Transjordan by proposing to him that he annex some of the Palestinian territory in the UN partition plan to his own kingdom. They happily encouraged King Abdullah to deepen his ties to the Zionist leadership in Palestine. It was with Britain's knowledge and tacit consent that King Abdullah came to an informal agreement with the Zionist leadership: if some of the Palestinian Arab territories were annexed to Transjordan, he would do his best to stand back from the Arab League's opposition to partition.

This was music to the Zionists' ears. In 1947, it was evident that an attempt to take over Palestine by force could prompt a formidable military reaction from the Arab world. The Zionist leadership needed a way to undermine the Arab military effort from the outset. The Arab Legion, Jordan's state army, was the most efficient army in the Arab world. It was the only army that had fought in the Second World War, in the Anglo–Iraqi War. All its senior officers were British, right up to the chief of the general staff, Sir

John Bagot Glubb. Neutralising this army, or even limiting its participation, would make it much easier for Zionists to transform Palestine into a Jewish state.

The complacency of the international community, the curious alliance that came together for the Zionist cause at the UN, and the way that a Jewish state was effectively treated as a fait accompli help explain the reactions that followed on the ground. Jewish settlers received the news with joy, even if the proposed partition was nowhere near what they wanted in theory. The fundamental point was that the highest international body had recommended creating a Jewish state. Meanwhile Palestinians heard the message loud and clear: self-determination didn't apply to them. Palestinians took to the streets to protest against the resolution, with the demonstrations turning violent in some cases. Yet after a few days, an uneasy calm prevailed. For both Palestinians and Zionists, it was time to prepare for a cataclysm. Knowing that Zionists were arming themselves, Palestinian politicians still on the ground felt that their existence was under threat. The Zionist paramilitary organisation Irgun, as well as targeting the British, attacked Arab villages to induce fear and encourage Palestinian Arabs to leave. Palestinians tried to organise paramilitary groups to defend their communities but the few weapons they had were of poor quality and even fewer had experience in wielding them. Anyone with a real gift for military organisation had already been killed or imprisoned during the 1936 Revolt. The Palestinian leadership hoped the

Arab League's volunteer force might offer more protection, but their hopes would be dashed.

At the end of the day, Palestinian youth formed two small paramilitary organisations, aided by a few hundred volunteers who managed to enter Palestine. Most of them were organised under a new body established by the Arab League, the Arab Liberation Army, led by Fawzi al-Qawuqji, an Iraqi officer with experience in the Arab Revolt.

But the Arab League decided not to send any regular troops before the end of the British Mandate, scheduled for 14 May 1948. The array of forces on the Palestinian side was no match for the three Zionist paramilitary groups: the Haganah, the Irgun and the Stern Gang. These groups were better equipped, had served in the British army, and, crucially, had at least ten times as many members. The international community, all signed up to a charter committed to the rule of law, justice and equal rights for nations, had cleared the road for a catastrophe – a catastrophe so all-encompassing it became the very definition of the Arabic word: *Nakba*.

# 8

# THE ETHNIC CLEANSING
# OF PALESTINE

As soon as a timescale had been set for British departure and the UN had endorsed partition as a 'solution' to the conflict, the Zionist leadership started planning its next steps. A small and highly clandestine group of advisers around the leader of the Jewish community in Palestine, David Ben-Gurion, started to sketch out how to establish dominance in the territory designated for the Jewish state – a territory where nearly half the population was Palestinian.

It was obvious from the moment that the UN voted for the resolution that the Palestinians and the Arab world would reject partition. Anticipating a war, Ben-Gurion and his collaborators were ready to contemplate taking over territories allocated to the Palestinian Arab state, after an assumed Zionist victory.

Between February 1947 and February 1948, the group gathered their forces and bided their time, confident that their planning would pay off. There were two stages to ensuring Jewish dominance, both numerically and in terms of sheer power, in the Jewish state Zionists were envisioning. In the first stage, Zionists exploited Palestinian outrage at the partition plan. When Palestinians attacked Jewish settlements, Zionists responded by collective punishment. They used Palestinian violence as an excuse to begin to clear Palestinian Arab areas of what would be the Jewish state; in other words, ethnic cleansing. In February 1948, the most brazen example of this kind of operation took place: in three villages around the ancient Roman city of Caesarea. These three villages were subject to such violent and forcible cleansing that hardly any of the buildings were left standing. It's almost impossible to find traces of the thriving communities they once were. Arab villagers were forced to leave en masse if they wanted to live. This was all done while the British were responsible for upholding law and order.

In the first two months of 1948, these experiments in ethnic cleansing were limited – they were always, however spuriously, justified by Zionist forces as a proportionate retaliation against Palestinian attacks on Jewish settlements and infrastructure. But by the end of February 1948, it was obvious that Zionist tactics were changing. Now Zionist forces were implementing mass expulsion operations, untethered from any notion of self-defence or response to Palestinian aggression.

The intensification of Zionist activity drew the attention of the US State Department, a long-time sceptic of Zionist colonisation. The UN partition plan did not seem plausible as a path towards peace anymore; it had proved to be a recipe for more violence. In an attempt to backtrack and allow time for a different solution to win consensus, on 19 March 1948, the American UN representative Warren Austin presented a proposal for Palestine to be under international trusteeship for five years. This was only a day after President Truman met with Chaim Weizmann, by now a quasi-elder statesman of the Zionist movement, and assured him of American support for partition.

The Zionist movement was predictably infuriated. It immediately mobilised its redoubtable lobby in the US. The lobby was helped by the fact it was an election year. A very aggressive campaign quickly bore fruit. Within a few weeks, the US administration made a hasty retreat from any gestures towards trusteeship and doubled down on their previous support for the partition plan.

## PLAN D

While the US was expressing hesitation about partition, the Zionist leadership in Palestine was moving forward with strengthening their position on the ground. They made the assessment that if they went ahead and built a Jewish state, any international objections would become immaterial.

On 10 March 1948, David Ben-Gurion and a small group of military generals in the Haganah's intelligence unit produced what would go down in history as Plan Dalet, or Plan D. As the name implies, it was the fourth such plan. But it was the one that would be implemented, with devastating consequences.

This plan was translated into direct orders to troops on the ground. Its aim was simple: to remove as many Palestinians as possible from Palestine, so a Jewish majority state could be forged. Here's the method: each village and neighbourhood was to be surrounded from three sides, leaving the fourth side free for residents to leave as they were expelled or fled in terror. Then the village was to be reduced to rubble, and explosives planted in the rubble, so no one could return. Where would all the Palestinians go? The plan was clear on this: they ought to leave the boundaries of the country.

In the master Plan D that was approved by the Zionist political leadership, Palestinians could avoid this treatment by unconditional surrender. But even then that excluded strategic locations. However, the actual orders sent to troops paid little mind to these delicate details. When we look at the actions of troops on the ground, it's obvious that Palestinian villages and neighbourhoods that the Zionists coveted were doomed to be ethnically cleansed from the start.

In the orders sent to troops, we find more harrowing details about the methods deployed. There was a reference to men, sometimes defined as being as young as ten years old, but usually between eighteen and forty-eight, who should be either killed or arrested.

We now know that this process was even more targeted, although the evidence does not appear in any official commands. In the 1940s, the Haganah's intelligence unit prepared files on every village in Palestine. They included extraordinarily detailed information on the village's wealth, from their internal relationships and political orientations, up to how many fruit trees they had. And each file had a list of people who took part in the 1936 Arab Revolt. If these people were still alive in 1948, they would be arrested or executed on the spot.

In the months of March, April and early May, the Zionist forces targeted the urban centres of Palestine. At the end of the day, they were all completely destroyed, in what we can only describe now as urbicide. In that period, the Palestinian population was expelled from Haifa, Bisan, Jaffa, Acre, Tiberias and Safed, as well as their surrounding villages. In many cases a massacre in a village preceded the military operation in the city; Zionist forces hoped it would accelerate flight and weaken resistance. The most notorious instance of such a tactic was in the cleansing of West Jerusalem and its thirty-nine neighbouring villages in April 1948. On 9 April 1948, right-wing paramilitary groups, the Irgun and the Stern Gang, stormed into the village of Deir Yassin and killed residents house by house, not even sparing women and children. Over one hundred villagers perished. Palestinians got the message, and many in the surrounding areas fled, fearing the advancing Jewish forces would do the same in their own villages

and neighbourhoods. Many members of these paramilitary groups would be integrated into the Israeli army after
independence, spearheaded by the Haganah.

## THE ARAB WORLD'S RESPONSE

By the official end of the Mandate, about 250,000
Palestinians were already refugees, some of whom made
their way into the neighbouring Arab states. This flow of
refugees put pressure on Arab governments to do more
for Palestine. Up until then, the Arab world had given
diplomatic support to the Palestinians, and allowed volunteers to try and enter Palestine to fight alongside the
Palestinians against the Zionist forces. But small bands of
volunteers were clearly no match for a well-organised and
well-funded military force that had been trained for this
occasion for years.

Arab states waited until 14 May 1948, i.e. the official
end of the Mandate, before they sent any troops to halt the
ethnic cleansing operations. By then, everything was too
little and too late. Why was this? Bluntly, Arab governments
like Lebanon and Syria, having achieved independence
only a few years prior, struggled to muster enthusiasm for
sending large armies to Palestine, while dealing with their
own internal power struggles.

The largest army was the Egyptian one, but even
this wasn't professional. Half of the troops were Muslim

Brotherhood volunteers, who saw the Palestinian cause as part of a broader anti-imperialist struggle. The Egyptian government would rather have avoided participating in a military operation altogether; it only authorised the deployment of troops two days before the end of the Mandate. Both their training and their equipment were lacking.

The most professional Arab army was Jordan's Arab Legion. But, as we saw, the government of Jordan had a behind-the-scenes agreement with the Zionist leadership. As 14 May 1948 approached, the main components of the secret agreement became clear. What we now know as the West Bank would be annexed by Jordan without a struggle. But the two sides hadn't come to an agreement on the fate of Jerusalem and the surrounding areas, and the Arab Legion fought for the city. Their bravery there stands in stark contrast to the way Jordanian forces passively watched Palestinian villages being destroyed elsewhere.

King Abdullah had to walk a tightrope between his agreement with Israel and his commitment to take part in the Arab League effort to save the Palestinians. So Abdullah privately negotiated with the Israelis while taking a leading role in planning the Arab military operations in Palestine. As a result of his double dealing, contrary to the plans drawn up by the Arab League under his direction, the Jordanian Arab Legion did not enter many parts of Palestine, and did not join forces with the Egyptian army in the south as planned.

Lacking proper logistical support, the Egyptian army halted after some initial success in occupying isolated Zionist settlements, even if this did not really help the Palestinians. By mid–August 1948, the all-Arab effort, including both regular troops and volunteers under the banner of the Arab Liberation Army, failed to prevent Israel's takeover of most of Palestine and the mass expulsions of Palestinians.

While these pan–Arab efforts were taking place, the ethnic cleansing of Palestine continued. As the Arab effort subsided, it accelerated. By the end of 1948, half of Palestine's Arab population had been expelled, more than five hundred villages were destroyed and most of its towns and cities had been demolished.

On the ruins, Israel built Jewish settlements and planted pine trees imported from Europe. Even more egregiously, some destroyed villages were turned into recreational parks. In this way, any lingering remnant of 'Arabness' was erased. A Jewish Palestine, in Zionist eyes, was to be a European Palestine.

Where did the expelled Palestinians go? Israel was able to expel the Palestinians in the east to the occupied West Bank and Transjordan. Those in the north were pushed into Syria and Lebanon. But in the south, Egypt refused to open its borders to Palestinians.

Towards the end of the war, Israel 'solved' this problem by creating what we now know all too painfully as the Gaza Strip. It was a small rectangle carved out of historical

Palestine (2% of the country). It was set up to receive the hundreds of thousands of Palestinians expelled by Israel from the central and southern areas of Palestine. It was the biggest refugee camp in the world then. It still is today.

It is hard to picture now, but at the time Gaza was a cosmopolitan town on the Via Maris, an ancient trade route that ran from Cairo to Damascus, and home to some of the oldest Christian and Jewish communities in the world.

## THE FIRST FAILED ATTEMPT
## AT PEACE, 1948-9

Israel perpetrated ethnic cleansing in plain sight of the world. As early as May 1948, the UN appointed a mediator, Count Folke Bernadotte, a Swedish diplomat, acclaimed for saving roughly 15,000 prisoners from concentration camps through negotiations with the Germans towards the end of the Second World War. He proposed revising the partition plan and adapting it to the demography as much as possible. He accorded more territory to the Arab state and demanded that expelled Palestinians be able to return to their former homes. Jerusalem, as in the original UN plan, would be an international enclave. Any proposal to limit the size of the Jewish state was completely unacceptable to the Zionist leadership. His diplomatic career came to an abrupt end. On 17 September 1948, he was assassinated by the Stern Gang; it was passed off as an act of terror by militants. But some historians suspect the official Zionist leadership was complicit, although the extent of this has never been established.

After his death, the UN once again reopened the question of how to end the conflict and find a solution both sides could live with. In December 1948, the UN passed, with a large majority, Resolution 194. This called for refugees to have the right of return, an international Jerusalem, and negotiations for a two-state solution on the basis of the borders set out in the 1947 Partition Resolution. To implement this resolution, it created a new body, the Conciliation Commission for Palestine.

This commission's main achievement was convening a peace conference in Lausanne, Switzerland, in April 1949, in which Israel, the Palestinians, Egypt, Syria, Lebanon and Jordan participated. Israel only took part grudgingly – its attendance was a precondition for its acceptance as a full member state of the UN. The US State Department, in the dying days of its influence on what was now considered the Arab–Israeli conflict, also exerted heavy pressure on Israel to attend. On 11 May, Israel became a full member of the UN.

One day later, all delegates at this conference signed the Lausanne Protocol. The protocol stated that everyone agreed to continue negotiations on the basis of three principles: the return of Palestinian refugees, the 1947 partition plan and the internationalisation of Jerusalem.

Israel swiftly disputed the claim that it had agreed to the protocol's terms as they were understood by everyone else. It was already unwilling to limit its borders to those outlined in the 1947 partition plan. Despite American pressure, which was short-lived, it was largely able to get away with this and negotiations drew to a halt. Within a year the Conciliation Commission effectively stopped looking for a solution. The only thing the UN really achieved was brokering a series of armistice agreements with Israel's Arab neighbours, and hence finalising Israel's borders.

This is what the international response to the ethnic cleansing of Palestine amounted to in the end. In 1950, one more body was founded: the United Nations Relief and Works Agency (UNRWA). This agency was meant to provide for nearly one million Palestinian refugees while they waited to return home. It built the refugee camps that are now a familiar part of cities such as Beirut, Damascus and Amman. Given the UN commitment to the right of return for refugees, refugees did not accept citizenship elsewhere, nor did they build new homes in their host countries. They did not want to imply that they were reconciled to their dispossession. In any case, many Arab countries like Lebanon did not offer the option of claiming citizenship. Jordan did, but only half of the refugee community there took it up.

Palestinians weren't only refugees in Arab countries. In the new state of Israel, there were also large numbers of refugees, usually near the destroyed villages upon which Jewish settlements were built. Israel refuses to deal with them as refugees, instead referring to them as internally displaced persons. Within Israeli borders they now number over 300,000. They are the most important link between the '48 Arabs, which is the way Palestinians refer to the Palestinian minority in Israel; and Palestinians scattered elsewhere, separated by borders, military force and decades of dispossession.

This is a significant point. The Nakba was not simply a land grab on the part of Zionist forces, but an attempt to make it impossible to reconstruct a Palestinian nation. The dispersion of Palestinians across so many different states, and the loss of age-old communities, has made it difficult to unify all the groupings into a single national movement. We will see how this played out later.

# 9

## AFTER THE NAKBA: ISRAEL
## AND PALESTINE, 1948–67

As we can see from the UN's half-hearted and ulti-mately futile attempts to prevent it through diplomatic means, Israel essentially got away scot-free with the ethnic cleansing of Palestine. No one condemned it for obvious crimes against humanity. This was not for lack of knowl-edge. Journalists, emissaries of the International Red Cross, representatives of the UN and others wrote frank, detailed reports about what was happening on the ground, narrating outbreaks of typhoid, malaria and scurvy. But these reports never got a wider public hearing, due to decisions taken by higher-ups.

Israel has an idiosyncratic understanding of international law and convention: what matters to it is how Israel's own political leaders interpret any individual position taken by the UN or another international body. The intentions of the international community simply don't count. Israel understood the silence and inaction during the Nakba as carte blanche to continue to use ethnic cleansing as a means of establishing and fortifying the Israeli state and its national security. After all, no one tried to stop them the first time round. The continued ethnic cleansing of Palestine since 1948, a process that goes on today, is called *al-Nakba al-Mustamirra* by the Palestinians, the Ongoing Nakba.

The repeated use of ethnic cleansing methods by Israel against the Palestinians further drew scholars to characterise it as a settler-colonialist society. As scholars of settler colonialism have argued, colonisation is not a one-off event – the simple conquest of land – but an ongoing structure to facilitate dispossession as long as the settler-colonial project is alive. The indigenous population has to remain in a subordinate position until native society has been destroyed, either through death or departure, or the colonisers withdraw from the project and are willing, as the Whites were in South Africa, to be part of a decolonised country.

Ethnic cleansing continued within Israel between 1948 and 1967, including the destruction of several Palestinian villages, up until the Six-Day War broke out. Nonetheless, Palestinians became a sizeable minority within the Jewish state, constituting around 17% of the population. This would rise to 20% after Israel annexed East Jerusalem and the Golan Heights, as we will see.

## MILITARY RULE INSIDE ISRAEL, 1948–66

The expulsions of Palestinian citizens of Israel between 1948 and 1967 were part of a repertoire of repression deployed against Palestinians who remained. Israel placed Palestinians within its borders under military rule, a regime that lasted until 1966 in most places, but even endured up until 1967 in others.

The military regime was in fact a legacy of the British emergency regulations, giving an army absolute control over citizens' lives. These powers allowed the expulsion of people for no reason, banishing them from their homes, detaining them without trial, shooting at them and ransacking their businesses. We still see these tactics today in the West Bank and the Gaza Strip.

Israeli forces also imposed curfews, frequently not communicated in advance. One such curfew was imposed on the village of Kafr Qasim, on the border between Israel and the Jordanian West Bank in October 1956, on the eve of the Sinai War. The Sinai War was a failed attempt by Israel, France and Britain to topple Gamal Abdel Nasser, the president of Egypt, following the 1952 revolution.

Nasser had nationalised the Suez Canal, which had been under British control since its construction in the nineteenth century. He demanded the withdrawal of British forces from Egypt. Even worse in the eyes of the West, he assisted the Front de Libération Nationale, the Algerian anticolonial movement against the French. Israel perceived him to be a strong supporter of the Palestinian cause. It hoped that it could depose him in collaboration with Britain and France and install a pro-Western leader in his stead.

On the eve of this fiasco, Israeli security services claimed, on the basis of no evidence, that Palestinians inside Israel would revolt and side with the Egyptians. It proposed imposing a curfew on Palestinian villages near the borders, and Kafr Qasim was one such village. This was despite the fact that Kafr Qasim was on the Green Line, on the border of the Jordanian West Bank, nowhere near Egypt.

The curfew was imposed at 4.30 p.m. on Monday 29 October 1956. According to its terms, anyone – man, woman or child – outside after 5 p.m. would be shot. Of course, many villagers were at work in the fields in the afternoon, and had no way of knowing about the curfew. As they returned home after a day's work, the Israeli border police shot them, killing forty-nine people. The massacre is still an open wound in the history and memory of Israel's Palestinian minority.

## EVENTS IN THE REST OF HISTORICAL PALESTINE, 1948–67

As we've seen, Jordan annexed the West Bank during the 1948 war. Although the Arab League had officially resolved that any governance over any part of historical Palestine not falling within Israel's official borders would be a temporary administration until Palestine was free, Jordan's King Abdullah ignored this. He united the East and West Banks of the River Jordan, declaring himself the king of Jordan and Palestine. Some notable families in the West Bank welcomed the move, seeing it as pragmatic. But once the Palestinian national movement rose from the ashes, it saw the West Bank as territory it needed to liberate.

There were a few refugee camps in the West Bank; refugees still hoped to return home and there remained a strong sense of Palestinian national identity. But in the refugee camps in the Gaza Strip, the Palestinian nation reawakened in full force. The first acts of resistance began, as they also did in the West Bank, with refugees trying to retrieve whatever was left of their animals, crops and other possessions in the ethnically cleansed villages. The Israeli forces deployed a policy of shoot-to-kill against them. The next step was to form guerrilla units which targeted the Israeli army and civilians. They were called the *Fedayeen*, meaning 'those ready to sacrifice themselves' in Arabic.

As this activity became more co-ordinated, Israel retaliated by establishing a new elite military unit, Unit 101, under the command of Ariel Sharon. In one infamous act of retribution in 1953, after the Fedayeen killed three civilians in Israel, Unit 101 attacked Qibya, a village in the West Bank, killing at least sixty-nine people, and blew up forty-five houses, some with people still inside them.

These and similar activities intensified on the Gaza–Israel border in 1955, serving as a pretext for Israel to join Britain and France in the Sinai War. In this war Israel briefly occupied the Gaza Strip and the Sinai Peninsula, but it was forced to withdraw by the US and the USSR.

After 1956, the Fedayeen in Gaza made connections with new initiatives led by Palestinian students in exile in places like Egypt, Kuwait and Lebanon. By 1957, they had organised themselves informally in a group called Fatah, an inverted acronym in Arabic of 'the Palestinian National Liberation Movement'. On 1 January 1965, it hit the headlines with a sabotage operation against Israel, where it tried, but failed, to blow up part of the National Water Carrier. Israel had built a water carrier that diverted some of the water of the River Jordan, which would flow through the carrier to the south of Israel. The attempt at sabotage was condemned by the US and further heightened tensions on the Israeli–Syrian border.

The new rulers of the West Bank, the Hashemite dynasty in Jordan, tried to limit the ability of Palestinian refugees to cross the border to their former villages and prevent the Fedayeen from carrying out operations against Israel. Moreover, King Hussein, the grandson of King Abdullah, persisted in trying to negotiate with Israel to quell conflict on the border throughout the early 1950s, but to no avail. The Fedayeen and Israeli forces continued to clash.

King Hussein's attempt to Jordanise, so to speak, the West Bank did not work well and the population there remained solid in their Palestinian identity. It remained Palestinian even after 1957, when King Hussein suspected a coup attempt by pro-Nasser Arab nationalist units in the Jordanian armed forces, mainly drawn from the West Bank. In response, King Hussein put the West Bank under military curfew, banned political parties and instituted rigorous censorship.

Despite his hostility towards pan-Arabism, King Hussein nonetheless participated in a Nasser-led Arab League initiative to renew interest in the Palestinian liberation struggle. In Jerusalem in 1964, the Arab League convened the Palestinian National Council, which would establish the Palestine Liberation Organization (PLO). It was composed of the former political leaders of the Palestinian community in the Mandatory period.

Meanwhile, more radical Palestinians joined the leftist pan-Arab nationalist movement, the *Qawmiyah al-Arabiyah*, from which left-wing groups within the PLO would emerge after 1967, such as the Popular Front for the Liberation of Palestine (PFLP) and the Democratic Front for the Liberation of Palestine (DFLP). Others joined Communist parties, pan-Syrian parties and various branches of the Ba'ath Party (which advocated socialist pan-Arab unity). The latter, whose name means 'renaissance' in Arabic, would become the dominant political force in Syria and Iraq.

Most of the political activity by Palestinians, whether in the West Bank and the Gaza Strip or outside of Palestine, was done in the refugee camps. Despite the poverty and bitter conditions, this is where the Palestinian activists were able to provide education, welfare and solidarity. They did not win liberation, obviously. But they kept the cause of Palestine alive; they refused to give up on their claims for justice.

## THE ARAB JEWS

Before we move on, we should say something about the make-up of Israel, in particular the 650,000 Jews who arrived from the Arab and Muslim world. Before 1948, the Zionist leadership was not keen on Arab Jews, whom they thought of as basically Arab. In Zionist eyes, they would not aid in building a European outpost on Middle Eastern soil.

However, the Holocaust destroyed European Jewish communities, leaving the population at one-third of its previous size. Moreover, most of the Jews in the US and Britain did not emigrate to Israel – they were too comfortable at home. That meant that Zionists had to look east to populate their new Jewish state. But it was not easy to convince Arab Jews to leave countries in which they had, in many cases, been settled for centuries, if not millennia. They had prospered there, had little experience of anti-semitism, and felt as Arab as their neighbours. Zionists had to resort to an aggressive campaign of persuasion, often resorting to underhanded methods.

In the late 1940s and early 1950s, the Zionist movement primarily targeted the Iraqi Jewish community, one of the oldest continuous Jewish communities in the world, dating back to the Old Testament. How did the Zionist leadership get them to emigrate en masse?

First, the Israeli intelligence service, Mossad, conducted false flag terror operations to sow fear among the Jewish community, including planting bombs in synagogues and other community centres. Second, Israel made a secret agreement with Iraq's prime minister, Nuri al-Said, who happily passed legislation against Jews, spurring them to leave. He took this as an opportunity to seize their substantial property and capital.

A different tactic was used in Yemen. Yemeni Jews were much more religiously observant than Iraqi Jews. They were persuaded to come to Palestine as fulfilment of a Jewish messianic prophecy that connected their return with the beginning of the redemption of the Jewish people. They were told that in Palestine, Zionists were building a pious Jewish society. This was at the same time Israeli leaders like David Ben-Gurion described themselves as building a modern socialist state.

Later waves of immigration from North Africa, Syria and Lebanon followed after the Six-Day War in 1967. Over the two decades since Israel's founding, the Zionist state had succeeded in making the Arab world equate Zionism with Judaism. And accordingly, fearing persecution in their homes, Arab Jews left for Israel.

The Jewish community in Egypt is a particularly interesting case. Again, Jewish presence there had been established since before the advent of Christianity. Israel made life difficult for Egyptian Jews in 1954 when it recruited a handful of young members of the community to commit terrorist attacks against targets in Egypt that were associated with the West (such as libraries and cinemas). The hope was that this would damage Egypt's relationship with the West. The terrorists were caught, but it stoked tensions in Egypt, and most Jews left for Israel or the US, concerned about their safety in such a hostile climate. It has now become infamous as the Lavon Affair, after the minister of defence Pinhas Lavon, who ordered the acts but denied responsibility. The Affair undermined Israeli prime minister Moshe Sharett's attempt to broker peace with Egypt.

The veteran Zionist leadership regarded Jews arriving from Arab and Muslim countries as inferior, and wasn't afraid to show its contempt. Upon arriving in Israel, many Arab Jews were sprayed with DDT, in a purposeful humiliation ritual. Zionists thought these Jews needed to be de-Arabised. Authorities broke down large extended families into nuclear families, and made sure young children were educated only in Hebrew and indoctrinated into believing in the valour of the Israeli state, while deliberately keeping Arab Jews on the margins of society. Many of those who arrived, no matter what job they did in their home country, were resettled in poor border towns, next to the neighbouring Arab states, and, due to lack of options, were forced to take unskilled jobs. To be recognised as an equal by the European Jews who made up the Israeli elite, it was obvious one had to disavow one's Arab past wholly and utterly. This aggressive project has, in large part, succeeded. Today Arab Jews form one of the largest voting blocs for right-wing parties in Israel, and are often the most vociferous advocates for violence against Palestinians. They have proven themselves as the most unyielding partisans of Zionism – even if they still haven't achieved equality.

# 10

## ON THE ROAD TO THE
## SIX-DAY WAR, 1967

Israel likes to propagate the myth that it stands alone, surrounded by states that want to annihilate it, and that's why it needs virtually unlimited military aid. The Six-Day War in 1967 is seen as a case in point. But this isn't an accurate portrayal of Arab states' attitudes to Israel. In the 1950s, despite Egyptian president Gamal Abdel Nasser's support for the Palestinian cause, he was nonetheless willing to explore the possibility of an agreement with Israel, which would allow Egypt to have a land bridge to Jordan, the return of refugees and the creation of a Palestinian state next to Israel. However, he had no reliable partners on the Israeli side. He hoped for international intervention that would rectify the injustice done to the Palestinians and contain Israel's expansionism. Until the Suez Crisis of 1956, both the British Foreign Office and the US State Department were willing to consider this idea as a basis for negotiations. But after Nasser nationalised the Suez Canal, demanded British withdrawal and turned to Moscow for help, this initiative died, and the British, without American approval, colluded with France and Israel to try and topple Nasser, as we've seen.

Israeli participation in this failed operation planted fear in Nasser's mind that Israel wasn't planning on stopping there and would topple the Arab nationalist regimes that had been established in Syria and Iraq. To try and prevent this from happening, and to strengthen his status in the Arab world, in 1958 he managed to persuade the Syrian government to unite with Egypt as one republic. This was called the United Arab Republic (UAR), only lasting three years. But even after its disintegration, Egypt and Syria remained strategic allies, united by the fear of an imminent Israeli attack on Syria and a commitment to the liberation of Palestine. When Israel began its project of diverting the River Jordan's water to its National Water Carrier in the mid-1960s, it caused constant friction on the Israel–Syria border.

But even Jordan, still ruled by the Hashemite dynasty and a rival to the pan-Arab movements in Egypt and Syria, shared this apprehension of Israeli aggression. Eventually it signed a defence agreement with Egypt in May 1967.

It had good cause to be nervous. Jordan's border with Israel had become a battlefield. Since 1965, Fatah, the Palestinian guerrillas, launched operations from Jordan and the West Bank. This led to brutal retaliation from Israeli forces, crossing into Jordanian territory. In November 1966, Israeli forces descended on the village of Samu to attack Fatah and ended up clashing with the Jordanian army, killing fifteen soldiers and one pilot. This further set the region careening into an all-out war.

There was a genuine fear among the governments of Egypt, Jordan and Syria that Israel was planning an attack on Syria. Nasser decided to respond through brinkmanship tactics. This meant undertaking military manoeuvres in the hope that it would cause the international community to intervene once more in the future of post-Mandatory Palestine. For that purpose, he moved troops to the Sinai Peninsula, which had been demilitarised after 1956 under the supervision of the UN, and closed the Tiran Straits, which are located on the entrance from the Red Sea to the Gulf of Aqaba, leading to the Israeli port city of Eilat.

But Israel exploited this brinkmanship to implement a vision many of its leaders wanted to push forward: Greater Israel. Greater Israel was equivalent to all of historical Palestine, namely Israel, the West Bank and the Gaza Strip of today. All of it would be a Jewish state through and through. Within the highest echelons of the Israeli government, there was a Greater Israel lobby. It consisted of mainly ex-generals from the 1948 war and old ideologues of the Labour movement, all of whom lamented not conquering the whole of historical Palestine in 1948. They were supported by what was then a small group of religious Zionists, young pupils of a yeshiva in Jerusalem, called the Rabbi's Centre (*Mercaz Harav*); they were disciples of a rabbi called Zvi Kook, who taught them that colonising the West Bank and the Gaza Strip was God's will and a religious imperative.

This lobby had already tried several times to persuade the prime minister of Israel, David Ben-Gurion, in power until 1963, that violating the armistice agreement with Jordan and occupying the West Bank was justified. In 1958, the lobby claimed that Jordan was about to be taken over by a pro-Nasserite coup and it would be prudent for Israel to have a solid border on the River Jordan and control over the West Bank. A second major attempt occurred in 1960, when Nasser thought wrongly that Israel was on the verge of attacking Syria and took measures similar to the ones he undertook before June 1967: pouring troops into the Sinai Peninsula and closing the Tiran Straits. Israel recruited its reserve army and that sufficed to de-escalate tensions. Both attempts were foiled by David Ben-Gurion, the architect of the 1948 ethnic cleansing. Having overseen the expulsion of up to one million Palestinians in 1948, he had no desire to incorporate these Palestinian areas into a Jewish state.

But Ben-Gurion was ousted in 1963 from mainstream politics, and his successors were far more open to the idea of creating a Greater Israel. In fact, the government convened a special group of experts to make a plan for ruling the West Bank and the Gaza Strip in the eventuality that these two areas fell into Israel's hands. Michael Shaham, who presided over the military rule imposed upon Palestinian citizens, headed the team. The programme is hence known as the Shaham Plan. It was finalised between 1963 and 1964, including clear guidelines on how to set up a military legal system after the occupation to enable policing and control the population. This is exactly what happened in June 1967.

As a war would be a useful pretext for occupying the coveted territory, Israel made sure that all the exit points to avert war were not utilised. And there were several such points. The international community could have de-escalated the situation with enough will, but Israel was determined to exploit the tensions to launch a war that would enable it to take over the parts of historical Palestine it had failed to take in 1948.

Israel launched its co-ordinated attack on 5 June 1967, beginning with the destruction of the air forces of Egypt, Syria and Jordan. Within six days the Israeli army created a mini-empire, occupying the West Bank, the Gaza Strip, the Sinai Peninsula and the Golan Heights.

To understand the conflict, we don't need to examine the relationships between Israel and Egypt or Syria that developed after June 1967. We'll maintain our focus on historical Palestine. However, we should note that when Israel took the Golan Heights in the Six-Day War, it ethnically cleansed nearly one hundred villages in the area, expelling their inhabitants to Syria. Israel hence continued to colonise these areas using the same methods it had honed in 1948.

# II

# THE MAKING OF THE TWO BIGGEST PRISONS ON EARTH, 1967–2000

As becomes clear from Israel's actions from 1948 to 1967, the Zionist movement is an ongoing settler-colonial project, seeking as much land as possible, with as few native inhabitants as possible. Until 1967, Israel had only conquered 78% of historical Palestine, so had not achieved its objectives completely.

But the Six-Day War gave Israel control over all of historical Palestine. What would it do now? The thirteenth government of Israel sought to answer this question.

This was the most pluralist government Israel has ever had to date. Every Zionist party was represented in this government, and even the ultra-Orthodox religious parties were part of it. The unity of this seemingly bizarre coalition is why it could make strategic decisions that continue to determine the fate of Israel and Palestine right up to today. Luckily, the minutes of these government meetings were declassified by the Israeli state archives in recent years. So we know in acute detail the decisions taken then, and the justifications given.

But first let's define the problem once more from the perspective of settler colonialism. The areas occupied, in particular the West Bank, were deemed crucial by the thirteenth government. For some parts of the government, it was necessary to control the West Bank because the region was considered the heart of biblical Israel and thus 'the heart of the nation', where biblical towns such as Hebron and Bethlehem were located. For others it was a necessary territorial addition to Israel, in order to have the River Jordan as a strategic barrier against a possible eastern front in a future Arab–Israeli war. This is somewhat absurd – and you only need to glance at the map to see why. The River Jordan has an average width of thirty metres – no advancing army would have any difficulty crossing it.

However, there was an obvious problem. The West Bank and the Gaza Strip both had large Palestinian populations. How do you take over the territory without the people? In 1948, as we have seen, the solution was to ethnically cleanse the territories and prevent Palestinians from returning. Could the same be done in the wake of the Six-Day War?

The government decided the same methods couldn't be used. It took several decisions that would inform the Israeli strategy towards the West Bank and the Gaza Strip up until 2005.

The first decision the government made was to let the majority of Palestinians stay in the new occupied areas, only expelling a relatively small number, at least compared to

1948. In total, Israel removed roughly 300,000 Palestinians from the territories occupied in 1967, mainly from the refugee camps near Jericho, the old city of Jerusalem and the Greater Jerusalem area.

Second, the Israeli government made the choice not to grant Israeli citizenship to Palestinians in the occupied territories. This was more controversial within the administration – some ministers wondered how long someone could live as a subject of a government without any of the rights of citizenship. Moshe Dayan, the minister of defence, said bluntly that people could live like this for at least fifty years. In other words, they had no interest in the set-up being temporary.

In practice, we have learned that you can only deprive millions of people of citizenship, i.e. the right to have a say in the decisions that shape their lives, by systemic oppression. You can only maintain this kind of status quo by a system of policing and control that violates their basic civil and human rights. For that purpose, the emergency regulations used to control the Palestinian minority inside Israel until 1967 were applied to the West Bank and the Gaza Strip, just as the Shaham team had planned prior to the war. These regulations gave absolute power to the army to detain people without trial, to close businesses, schools and workplaces, to impose curfews and closures, and to expel people and harass civilians with impunity.

They made one more fundamental decision at these meetings. While Israel did not object to a peace process in principle, it would never include giving up control over the West Bank and the Gaza Strip. This has produced a very disingenuous Israeli position over the years, in particular in the Labour Party (in government 1969–77; jointly in the unity governments of 1984–90, 1992–6 and 1999–2001). Israeli governments claim to agree to be part of a peace process that would discuss the fate of the West Bank and the Gaza Strip but in practice they do not envisage an Israel that does not have direct or indirect control over these areas. The Israeli government holds this position to this day, and has in fact only doubled down on it over the decades.

The thirteenth unity government of 1967 was replaced by Labour-dominated governments that ruled Israel for the next eight years (1969–77). While these were in power, the official Israeli position was known as the 'Jordanian option', proposed by the Labour politician Yigal Allon, a long-term believer in the Greater Israel. Under the terms of this plan, Israel would cede control over certain parts of the West Bank to Jordan, and take over the rest. This would allow the Jordanians to annex the areas most populated with Palestinians and leave the less dense areas, even if they were adjacent to the border with Jordan, in Israeli hands.

While nothing came of it, Allon pushed for Jews to settle in the West Bank areas he identified as belonging to Israel. This is how the Labour Party created the first, illegal, Jewish settlements in the Jordan Valley near Hebron, Bethlehem and the Greater Jerusalem area. Allon was also responsible for the first attempt to expel the Palestinians from the south Hebron mountains, an area called Masafer Yatta, for the sake of establishing Jewish territorial integrity from the Negev to the River Jordan. The Palestinians there resisted, and they still resist ethnic cleansing in this region today. After the events of 7 October 2023, while everyone's eyes were on Gaza, Jewish settlers in that area, with the full collaboration of the Israeli army, succeeded in expelling thousands of Palestinians from their villages there.

But the problem for the Labour Party was that settlers had their own ideas about where they wanted to live, not restrained by any diplomatic niceties. A new messianic movement of Jews, who would become Gush Emunim (Bloc of the Faithful) in 1974, would bring thousands of Jews into the West Bank and the Gaza Strip. Their slogan ran: 'the land of Israel for the people of Israel according to the Torah of Israel'.

Gush Emunim settled precisely in the places the Allon plan would have ceded to Jordan. They used a 'biblical map' – which pointed to the most densely populated Palestinian areas of the West Bank as the targets of their settlement. They sought to make the Jewish settlements a fait accompli, and the government let them.

All these settlements were and are illegal according to the conventions of international law, most importantly the Geneva Convention. According to the Fourth Geneva Convention, states are not allowed to transfer their citizens to the occupied area, and they are not allowed to take the land of occupied people by force. When human rights organisations tried to challenge the settlements in their early stages, the Israeli Supreme Court authorised the settlements by claiming that they were temporary and only for defence and national security purposes. Later the same Supreme Court legalised the transformation of these 'military' outposts into civilian settlements. Israel hence claims it's in the clear – but international law remains unchanged.

New settlements in the Gaza Strip started as early as 1968. Under the premiership of Yitzhak Rabin, in his first term between 1974 and 1977, the Labour Party also encouraged the settlement of Jews in the Gaza Strip, creating what would become Gush Katif, a dense concentration of Jewish settlements in the Strip.

The Gaza Strip had been an invention of the Israelis in 1948, faced with a seemingly intractable refugee problem. But despite the efforts of Allon and other Greater Israel visionaries, after 1967 the Israeli government managed to settle only a few thousand there. Many more settled in the Sinai Peninsula occupied by Israel, leading Israel to build two new towns there. Their inhabitants would be evicted after 1979 when Israel made peace with Egypt.

Judaisation efforts were not limited to the West Bank and the Gaza Strip under the Labour government. Half of the Palestinian citizens in Israel lived in the region of Galilee, and they made up half of the territory's population. Israel wanted to shift the demographic balance dramatically to put Jews in the majority position. While efforts had been made sporadically since 1948, in 1976, the Labour government spearheaded the project of the 'Judaisation of Galilee'. It confiscated Arab lands, and built new military bases and new Jewish settlements.

The Palestinian community in Galilee had no illusions about what was going on. To protest against the ongoing theft of their land, they announced a day of strike action in March 1976. Israel reacted ruthlessly, killing six Palestinian citizens. This day has become the 'Day of the Land', commemorated every year by Palestinians in Israel and in the occupied territories.

## INTERNATIONAL IMMUNITY FOR THE OCCUPATION

Immediately after the Six-Day War, the US assumed responsibility for efforts to 'resolve' the conflict. Before 1967, the US had remained aloof from any diplomatic efforts to change the reality on the ground in historical Palestine, not seeing it as their remit.

In fact, until the assassination of President John F. Kennedy in November 1963, American diplomatic interventions on the issue weren't co-ordinated with Israel on the rare occasions when they took place, and at times, although the US administration claimed to be generally supportive of Israel, America's positions clashed with

Israel's actions and desires. Until 1963, the American government was still supporting Palestinian refugees' right of return, was not enthusiastic about the Israeli diversion of the River Jordan and occasionally condemned excessive Israeli retaliation operations in Jordanian and Syrian sovereign territory against the Palestinian guerrilla movement. The US also refused to help Israel to build nuclear capacity; Israel had to turn to France for this favour.

However, in 1963, AIPAC (the American Israel Public Affairs Committee), a formidable pro-Israel lobby group, was incorporated. It built an extensive political machine that made sure the huge majority of American politicians would lend Israel unconditional support. So even if the administration was uncomfortable with Israel's policies, this would never be translated into any meaningful action.

The final futile condemnation from the US came after the Six-Day War ended, when Israel officially annexed East Jerusalem. Even in 1949, the US had joined other countries in condemning the Israeli decision to make West Jerusalem its capital, and hence violating the terms of the UN's Partition Resolution, which envisaged Jerusalem being an international city. And so, right up until Donald Trump's presidency, the US embassy was in Tel Aviv and not Jerusalem.

But after the 1967 war, the US adopted a different strategy that still informs its priorities today. The strategy was based on the view that the conflict had begun in 1967, that it was not Israel's fault, and that it would be generous for Israel to concede some territories for the sake of peace. The basis for this strategy was UN Security Council Resolution 242, responding to the 1967 war. In one version of Resolution 242, it called upon Israel to withdraw from all the occupied territories and to rec- ognise the territorial integrity of its neighbours, as the precondition for peace. In what was swiftly becoming typical behaviour of Israel, it insisted that this only meant withdrawal from some of the territories.

The UN would also reiterate the same principle fol- lowing the Yom Kippur War in October 1973, in which Egypt and Syria attacked Israel with the goal of winning the occupied Golan Heights. Israel repelled the attack with the assistance of the US, leading to a long truce that would ulti- mately result in a peace treaty between Israel and Egypt. UN Security Council Resolution 338 called for the implemen- tation of Resolution 242, and paid lip service to the rights of Palestinian refugees, those from both 1948 and 1967.

Before the Yom Kippur War, this American strategy, derived from UN Resolution 242, was also endorsed by the European Economic Community. The US didn't implement it in a uniform and consistent way; it varied depending on the personality of the president at the time. Obviously an Obama strikes a different tone to a Trump.

During the Richard Nixon administration (1969–74), the US became involved in the first attempts to push forward a solution based on Resolution 242. As secretary of state, William Rogers attempted to realise the eponymous Rogers Plan for peace, entailing Israeli withdrawal from Egyptian territories, and lasting peace between Israel and Egypt. He ignored the question of Palestine. But he was outmatched by Nixon's national security adviser, Henry Kissinger, who would later assume Rogers's post as secretary of state.

This endeavour failed; a failure that led to the Yom Kippur War in 1973.

There was an alternative attempt advocated in the UN by Arab and African countries which proposed a very different approach to the problem in historical Palestine. The newly decolonised countries, especially from Africa, were united in helping the Blacks in South Africa in their struggle against the apartheid regime. They felt that Israel was another apartheid state that had to be resisted in the same way. In their eyes the African National Congress (ANC) and the Palestine Liberation Organization (PLO, founded in 1964 as an umbrella body for all Palestinian resistance groups) were both legitimate anticolonialist movements. In 1975, these member states were able to pass a resolution in the UN General Assembly that stated Zionism 'is a form of racism and racial discrimination'. This resolution would stand until 1991, when a new resolution, spearheaded by the US, revoked it. It was part of the diplomatic front in the PLO's two-pronged strategy for the liberation of Palestine, alongside armed struggle.

The willingness of the PLO to enter into negotiations gained wider legitimacy for the organisation throughout Europe. PLO legations opened up across the world. But the PLO did not give up guerrilla warfare, sometimes to its own detriment. One of its operations that backfired was the abduction of the Israeli delegation to the 1972 Munich Olympics, carried out by the militant affiliate Black September. Eleven Israeli members of the delegation lost their lives in a botched attempt to rescue them by the German police. Israel retaliated by assassinating PLO leaders in Europe and the Arab world over a period of twenty years, in what they called Operation Wrath of God.

Six years later, Fatah undertook another operation: hijacking a bus heading to Tel Aviv from Haifa, killing thirty-seven civilians. This time Israel responded by occupying the south of Lebanon, the base for the PLO since 1970. It wanted to destroy all PLO infrastructure there. Until 1970 the PLO headquarters and main forces were concentrated in the Palestinian refugee camps in Jordan. However, the Hashemite rulers felt threatened by the PLO and its component groups using Jordanian territory as a base to launch attacks into Israeli soil. In September 1970, the Jordanians decided to act against the presence of the PLO in Jordan and began a ruthless military campaign against them, culminating in the PLO moving headquarters to Beirut and south Lebanon. In south Lebanon, volunteers from many parts of the world joined the Palestinian groups in guerrilla training. By 1978, Israel was none too happy about its opponents having eight years of guerrilla training under their belt and so launched Operation Litani, named after the river thirty kilometres away from the Israel–Lebanon border.

Israel occupied south Lebanon up to the River Litani and directly intervened in the Lebanese Civil War, raging since 1975. In Lebanon, Sunni Muslim militias, leftist groups, right-wing Maronite Christians known as Phalangists, and a Shia militant group called Amal (the predecessor to Hezbollah) fought for control of the country. The PLO and Syria had already taken sides. In the array of forces that emerged, the PLO and the Maronite Phalangists were in rival camps. When Israel decided to invade south Lebanon, it aligned itself with a Maronite South Lebanese Army, under the command of Major Haddad, with soldiers drawn from the Maronite and Shia communities in the south of Lebanon.

The South Lebanese Army de facto ran the south of Lebanon for Israel, replacing the PLO as the armed force there. But the PLO continued its struggle, and by 1981, the border between Lebanon and Israel became a battlefield once more. Nonetheless, through American mediation, a truce was agreed by both sides in early 1982. But it didn't last long. Within a few months Israel would violate its terms.

## SHARON'S WAR AGAINST THE PALESTINIANS, 1981–2

This relapse into war came down to the decisions of an ambitious new minister of defence, Ariel Sharon, appointed by the right-wing government of Menachem

Begin (1977–83). He was fixated on annexing both the West Bank and the Gaza Strip, whether officially or not. This was not his first brush with the Palestinians, as we've seen. In 1953, he headed up Unit 101, which perpetrated the notorious Qibya massacre. As the general commander of southern areas of Israel, he conducted a merciless campaign of repression against Palestinians in Gaza who were engaged in resistance activities between 1968 and 1970.

Although his career flourished in regions normally associated with Israel's Labour Party, in 1977 he helped Menachem Begin to establish a significant right-wing political bloc, the Likud, advocating the creation of a Greater Israel, i.e. annexing the West Bank and the Gaza Strip.

Even before he became minister of defence, he was the dynamo behind the expansion of the Jewish settlements in the West Bank in his previous governmental positions. When he entered the ministry of defence, he replaced military rule with a civil administration, imposed on the West Bank and the Gaza Strip in 1981. The civil administration was run by Israel as a quasi-government of the occupied territories; it drove Israel one step further on the path to annexation. In practice, it made the lives of Palestinians even more miserable, adding harassment by a hostile bureaucracy to the humiliation of military oppression. As a Palestinian in the West Bank or the Gaza Strip, you could not move about, have a job, go to university or attend a hospital without obtaining the necessary permits from the civil administration.

These permits would be examined at checkpoints. These became the bane of Palestinians' daily existence. Soldiers bullied, abused and persecuted Palestinians as a matter of course. The Israeli security service used the checkpoints to exert pressure on Palestinians to collaborate as informers or be refused the permits they needed.

The local Palestinian leadership under occupation responded in 1978 by creating a national committee, *Lajnat al-Tawjih* (the 'committee of guidance' in Arabic). It sought non-violent means of ending the occupation, but its leaders were arrested by the Israeli army and attacked by Jewish settlers.

But this was not enough for Sharon. He first tried to establish an alternative Palestinian leadership, called the 'Villages' League', which would be loyal to Israel, but this was unsuccessful. The leadership in the West Bank and the Gaza Strip at the time was loyal to the PLO as the only representative of the Palestinian people that was willing to discuss a two-state solution, and demanded the return of refugees.

The PLO headquarters at that time was in Lebanon. Despite the Israeli occupation of the south of Lebanon in 1978, it still exercised a strong influence on the politics of the Palestinians wherever they were. Sharon believed that he was unable to nurture an alternative Palestinian leadership because of the PLO's influence.

Sharon was looking for a pretext not only to destroy the PLO in Lebanon but to install a pro-Israel government in Lebanon. The opportunity arose on 4 June 1982, when the Abu Nidal group, unaffiliated to the PLO, attempted to assassinate the Israeli ambassador in London, Shlomo Argov. Two days later, Israel began what it called Operation Peace for Galilee, otherwise known as the First Lebanon War. This was Sharon's gambit to bring an end to the Palestinian resistance. But it failed.

The Israeli army managed to occupy much of Lebanon, including the capital Beirut. In this it was assisted by the Phalangists, the right-wing Maronite militia who hoped that Sharon would help them to gain more power in Lebanon. And with Israel's help, a president from their group, Bashir Gemayel, was elected for a short while, on a platform of peace with Israel. This alliance also enabled the Phalangists to massacre thousands of Palestinians in two refugee camps, Sabra and Shatila, in September 1982.

The Israeli army imposed a siege on Beirut and incessantly bombarded it. Under the leadership of Yasser Arafat, the PLO surrendered and agreed to move their headquarters to Tunis. They left Lebanon in September 1982. The Israeli army withdrew from Beirut back to the south of Lebanon.

Then and there a new resistance struggle commenced against the Israeli occupation of south Lebanon, led by a new Shia group, Hezbollah. After a long guerrilla war, in

2000, Hezbollah forced the Israeli army to withdraw from Lebanon altogether.

The disempowerment of the PLO, after it was removed to Tunis, affected its ability to continue the struggle for the liberation of Palestine. In an attempt to make the best of bad circumstances, the PLO decided to work closely with Jordan – despite the kingdom's unreliability – and be part of the American peace effort. But there was no willingness on the Israeli side to reach an agreement on the future of the occupied territories with either Jordan or the PLO.

# 12

# BETWEEN TWO INTIFADAS, 1987–2000

By 1987, the people in the occupied territories had had enough of twenty years of forced expulsions, arrests, lengthy and unexplained detainments and abuse becoming their routine. They were not going to wait around for a chastened PLO to lead them in their liberation struggle. In December 1987, after an Israeli truck collided with a civilian car in Gaza, the First Intifada ('uprising' in Arabic) erupted. It was mainly a non-violent protest movement, in which the Palestinians were able to control villages and neighbourhoods and run them on the basis of solidarity and self-sustainability for a short time. The Israeli army reacted with full force. Notoriously the then minister of defence, Yitzhak Rabin, ordered soldiers to 'break the bones' of the protestors. There were widespread demonstrations in solidarity with the uprising among the Palestinians inside Israel.

The uprising continued up until 1993. Israel killed over one thousand Palestinians, detained people without trial and deployed measures of collective punishment: home demolitions, curfews, school closures and expulsions.

The situation became somewhat more complicated in the early 1990s in the wake of Saddam Hussein's invasion of Kuwait. The chairman of the PLO, Yasser Arafat, decided to support Saddam, while most of the Arab world condemned the invasion. The PLO became further isolated on the international stage as a consequence of this decision. It also lost the main superpower support it had enjoyed throughout the decades: the USSR collapsed, leaving Russia in an internal crisis.

But there was a silver lining to the First Gulf War. The US responded to the invasion of Kuwait by forming an international military coalition to force the Iraqi army to withdraw from Kuwait. Arab countries agreed to participate on the condition that the US would convene an international conference which would seek a solution to the Palestine question.

Palestinians were more hopeful about this conference than previous efforts, because this time they would be included in the negotiations over the future of Palestine. Even as early as the late 1980s, before the invasion of Kuwait, the US was willing to open direct negotiations with the PLO in Tunis, sensing that the organisation and its leader were very keen to be part of a Pax Americana. They knew that Arafat was prepared to recognise Israel and renounce armed struggle, or, as the US and Israel described it, terrorism. What Americans could not foresee was that even such dramatic steps would not persuade Israel to halt its colonisation of the West Bank and Greater

Jerusalem. Nor was Israel willing to enter into any serious negotiations for a two-state solution. Whether it was Likud or Labour in power, the Israeli government had no inclination whatsoever to give up the territory won in the 1948 and 1967 wars. Israel had effectively taken over all of historical Palestine, and removed millions of Palestinians from their homes. For successive Israeli administrations, this was the prime achievement of the Jewish state.

## THE MADRID CONFERENCE, 1991

So, motivated by the PLO's conciliatory attitude, the US and USSR, in its dying days, convened the peace conference at the end of October 1991 in Madrid.

The US forced Israel to participate in this conference; this kind of pressure was one of the hallmarks of the new American approach. It faced the intransigent prime minister Yitzhak Shamir, leading a Likud government after the dissolution of Israel's unity government (1984–8). Israel only agreed to attend if the PLO would not be officially present. It is worth dwelling on the absurdity here – Israel would only attend provided they did not have to negotiate with the Palestinians. A compromise was reached: two Palestinian delegations arrived in Madrid. One was from the West Bank and the Gaza Strip and was part of the official Jordanian delegation. The other delegation had no formal role; it came from Tunis and represented the PLO.

The members of the first delegation prepared for the conference meticulously. They were led by people such as Haidar Abdul Shafi from the Gaza Strip, Faysal Husayni from Jerusalem and Hanan Ashrawi from Ramallah. Behind them was the hard work of teams of Palestinian experts (the *Tawaqim*), toiling away in Orient House in Jerusalem, planning the infrastructure for an independent Palestinian state in the West Bank and Gaza Strip.

Orient House belonged to Jerusalem's most important notable family, the Husaynis. After the Six-Day War in 1967, it became the informal headquarters of the Palestinian national movement, and was subject to regular repression by the Israeli government. In 1988, for instance, it was closed entirely. But the Husayni family continued to support the Palestinian national movement and convene these teams. Their plans laid the political and social foundations for a genuine two-state solution. Had the Israelis been prepared to compromise then, two states may have developed as a feasible solution.

But the ideas of the Palestinian delegates were totally rejected by the Israelis, even if the US State Department found them impressive. It was not only the Israelis who rejected the work of the Palestinian teams based in Jerusalem. The PLO leadership in Tunis felt it was losing its hold on being the sole political representative of the Palestinians. Israel and the PLO hence went behind the scenes to conduct talks between themselves. The Madrid

Peace Conference ended in complete failure. It was dominated by a paradigm of 'conflict resolution' that ignored the actual causes of the conflict. Emblematic of this was the decision to postpone discussion about the status of Jerusalem and the right of return of refugees indefinitely: two crucial bones of contention.

## THE OSLO I ACCORD, 1993

In 1992, the Labour Party returned to power in Israel under the leadership of Yitzhak Rabin. Palestine was not initially a priority for Rabin; he was more interested in peace with Syria. He thought that could clear the way later for peace with the Palestinians.

His eternal nemesis, the foreign minister Shimon Peres, with the help of his deputy, Yossi Beilin, preferred to try the Palestinian track first. They made the correct assessment that the PLO in Tunis lacked the fortitude of the Palestinian leadership based in Orient House, and was much more willing to make concessions. And so Peres began direct negotiations with the PLO in Tunis, without the knowledge of the prime minister.

The Labour Party in Israel had a good working relationship with the Labour Party and trade unions in Norway, as did the PLO. So Fafo, a non-profit institute originally founded by the Norwegian Confederation of Trade Unions, was a natural choice for a mediator.

Fafo's past record and philosophy suited the Israelis very well. It drew upon the prevailing theories of conflict management in the Western social sciences. In simple terms, it looked at conflicts in terms of the imbalances of power, and working out who the stronger party was. In the Israel–Palestine conflict, this is self-evidently Israel. The mediator's role is to get the best offer from the stronger party and then pressure the weaker side to accept it. In such a framework, the demands of the weaker party don't count for much at all. Their role is simply to accept whatever scraps they are given by the stronger party. The assumption underpinning these 'negotiations' is that what's offered is enough of an improvement on the present reality that the weaker party will be prepared to accept it, regardless of how far it falls short of what they actually want.

In essence, this was the framework guiding the Oslo I Accord signed on 13 September 1993 on the White House lawn. A disempowered PLO, now bereft of the former USSR, condemned in some Arab countries for Arafat's support for the Iraqi invasion, and conscious of the rise of an alternative Palestinian leadership in the occupied territories, agreed, on paper, to accept the Israeli diktat.

The Israelis were willing to give up direct control over about 40% of the West Bank and allow a new body created by the Oslo I Accord, the Palestinian Authority, to manage domestic affairs for the Palestinians. But it would have to agree to collaborate with the Israeli army and secret services in monitoring and suppressing any resistance to the occupation. The old PLO metamorphosed into the new Palestinian Authority (the PA), and the PLO's leader, still Yasser Arafat, became the president of the PA. The Accord also provided for a new institution, the Palestinian Legislative Council, as the parliament of the PA. This would work in parallel to the Palestinian National Council – the main decision-making body of the PLO. The duplicity of the PLO, going behind the backs of most of the resistance, hindered the development of a clear, united Palestinian strategy. Some of the key figures and organisations in the resistance, that were part of the PLO, rejected the Oslo I Accord and refused to participate in the PA. Interestingly, left-wing groups did join it. This was a key turning point for the Palestinian resistance, which up until then was dominated by a broadly secular, left-wing leadership. Political Islamist groups, Hamas and Palestinian Islamic Jihad, did not join the PA and refused to organise themselves under the banner of the PLO. They did not accept the Oslo I Accord. The resistance movement was hence clearly split.

Now, of course, in many Western eyes, Hamas in particular is practically synonymous with the Palestinian resistance. Let's examine its origins to explain how it rose to such prominence. Hamas is an acronym in Arabic for 'Islamic Resistance' (*Harakat al-Muqawama al-Islamiya*). It grew out of the Palestinian branch of the Muslim Brotherhood, founded in Egypt in 1928. This movement emerged as a reaction to two major developments in the

interwar period: a sense that Western powers were contin-
uing to exert too much cultural and economic influence
and the failure of the secular national movements to
deliver genuine independence and tackle the entrenched
problems of poverty, unemployment and poor housing.
Hassan al-Banna, a charismatic schoolteacher, convinced
workers that the best way to address these issues was an
Islamic revival. In Egypt the Brotherhood initially focused
on providing social services, such as schooling and healthcare. But for many of its adherents it transformed into
a political vision for an Islamic state that would implement Sharia law. This was counterposed to Western state
models that seemed to leave too many hungry and out
of work.

The Muslim Brotherhood branch in the Gaza Strip also
encompassed both these tendencies: those seeking solidarity in their piety and those who thought the liberation
of Palestine could only be won on Islamic terms.

After the Israeli occupation of Gaza and the West Bank,
the Israeli authorities had a positive attitude towards the
Muslim Brotherhood. They thought it could drive a wedge
among Palestinians and hence weaken the secular Fatah
movement, then actively trying to liberate the occupied
territories and Palestine more generally. So they allowed it
to gain influence in the Strip.

In December 1987, shortly after the outbreak of the
First Intifada, the Muslim Brotherhood made the decision
to set up an armed wing: what we now all know as Hamas.

Its leader, Sheikh Ahmed Yassin, openly called for the founding of an Islamic state in Palestine and for a struggle against Israel – principles that appeared in Hamas's charter in 1988. However, for Israel, Hamas was still a useful counterbalance against the secular and left-wing forces in the resistance movement. Israel's history of covert support stands in stark contrast to its histrionic declarations today that Hamas is no better than ISIS.

Palestinian Islamic Jihad was also born out of the Muslim Brotherhood movement but was founded earlier – in 1981 – inspired by the Islamic Revolution in Iran. It remains closely associated with the Islamic Republic of Iran today.

Both movements had a military wing and a political one. Many countries in the West officially consider both as terrorist organisations. But despite the West's condemnations, they remain part of the anticolonialist Palestinian liberation movement.

## OSLO II: A NEW KIND OF OCCUPATION

In September 1995, the vague principles of the Oslo agreement were translated into a more detailed agreement, the Oslo II Accord.

It was signed in Taba near the border between Israel and Egypt, and broadcast live to interested viewers. And so millions saw the moment that Arafat was literally pushed by the Egyptian president to sign the Accord. He had good reason to be hesitant, as we'll see.

The Israelis implied, although they refused to explicitly commit to it, that the Palestinian area that would be governed autonomously according to the Oslo agreements could become a state. But it was clear that whatever form it took, it could not function without Israel's cooperation and overarching control. The area allocated to the Palestinians in the Oslo II Accord was defined as Area A. It included the more densely populated parts of the West Bank, but constituted no more than 18% of the West Bank.

Two other areas were defined by Oslo: Area B, where Israel and the Palestinian Authority formally shared power, but Israel of course was the effective ruler; and Area C, where most of the Israeli Jewish settlements were. Palestinian access to Area C was restricted. The Gaza Strip remained undefined, but was run along similar lines to Area B.

The Palestinians were offered Ramallah as their capital and there was no real discussion about the Palestinian refugee problem. Israel paid some lip service to discussing Jerusalem and the settlements in the future, as a reward for Palestinian 'good behaviour'.

Initially, at least from the perspective of the PLO, this seemed fair enough. Its leaders, including Arafat, were allowed to return to Palestine and establish Palestinian institutions that would be the basis of a future Palestinian state. It is also possible that some of them, including Arafat, hoped to continue the struggle for liberation from within.

Up until November 1995, the Palestinian leadership and many ordinary Palestinians accepted Oslo II as a good start – and something that could be improved later on. But developments on the ground meant that any further concessions to the Palestinians were not to be. At the end of the day, Oslo II produced a reality in the occupied territories that was far worse than what came before it.

The unresolved questions about the settlements led to unprecedented violence by Jewish settlers. Palestinian resistance factions, opposed to Oslo altogether, responded by striking at civilian targets, including Israeli buses and shopping malls. In turn, the Israeli army would collectively punish the Palestinian population. Oslo seemed to have set off cycles of violence – it did not appear to be bringing any peace.

Moreover, right-wingers in Israel fervently opposed the Oslo Accords and wanted no concessions made at all to Palestinians. In November 1995, just two months after Oslo II was signed, the Israeli prime minister Yitzhak Rabin was assassinated. Now the entirety of Israeli politics moved rapidly to the right.

Rabin's natural successor in the Labour Party, Shimon Peres, could not win the subsequent elections. A brutal terror attack by an extreme right-wing Jew was simply not enough to prevent Israel's shift to the right.

And so Benjamin Netanyahu, the leader of the right-wing Likud, won his first election as Israel's prime minister. It would be one of many. He vowed to honour the Oslo Accords but in practice his government implemented ever more oppressive measures against the Palestinians. Hundreds of checkpoints were built between Areas A, B and C, between the north and south of the Gaza Strip and between the occupied territories and Israel.

As we've seen, these checkpoints were the site of routine degradation for Palestinians. Israeli forces had no qualms about flagrantly breaching Palestinians' basic rights, and abusing civilians for no reason at all. At times of heightened tensions, human rights organisations reported on mothers who had to give birth near the checkpoints, unable to reach hospitals, and patients dying for the same reason. Normal life was made impossible: whether you made it to school, your job or back home for dinner all depended on the whims of the soldiers at the checkpoint that day. In 1996, Netanyahu's administration built a barbed wire fence around the Gaza Strip. It now resembled a prison more than anything else.

Moreover, the new Likud government intensified the Judaisation of the Greater Jerusalem area, openly allowing Jewish settlers to dispossess Palestinians. It invented pretexts to force Jerusalemite Palestinians to move to the West Bank and designated particular neighbourhoods in Jerusalem, not originally part of Area C, as 'West Bank villages', thereby making them part of Area C.

Any resistance was met with brutal collective punishment. Early on in Netanyahu's tenure after Israel built tunnels alongside the Western Wall in Jerusalem, mass Palestinian protests broke out in both the West Bank and Gaza Strip. During the protests, fifty-nine Palestinians were killed. The Americans, realising that the situation was reaching crisis point, attempted to re-instigate the 'peace process'. In 1998, they tried to reconcile Netanyahu and Arafat.

In Maryland in 1998, Arafat and Netanyahu signed the Wye River Memorandum – an agreement that would never be implemented. It was entirely detached from reality. The agreement envisaged that in exchange for moving a small part of Area C and an even smaller part of Area B into Area A, Palestinians would give up any and all resistance to the occupation. Israel thought even this was far too generous. Area C, under direct Israeli rule, consisted of more than 70% of the West Bank then. It still does today.

A more limited agreement, also unrealised, was signed about the future of the city of Hebron, the commercial capital of the West Bank. To understand why Hebron was so contentious, we'll need to go back to the two rival ideologies driving Jewish colonisation of the West Bank, especially the messianic Zionists of Gush Emunim.

As we've seen, there were two maps for Jewish colonisation of the West Bank. One, proposed by the Labour Party, avoided settling in areas densely populated by Palestinians, and one prepared by the new messianic movement, Gush Emunim aimed to settle in the most densely populated Palestinian areas – as they were places of significance in the Old Testament. In Hebron the two maps worked in tandem. Next to Hebron the Labour government built a new city, Kiryat Arba, hosting, among others, many disciples of Rabbi Meir Kahane, an American Jew gaining popularity for his call to transfer all the Palestinians out of Israel and the occupied territories. In the old city of Hebron, a messianic group settled. With the help of zealots from Kiryat Arba, they expanded their presence into the very heart of Hebron. They moved into new neighbourhoods through an open policy of naked aggression and violence while the army turned a blind eye. It led to the almost total de-Arabisation of the old city. Only a small group of courageous Palestinians remains, subject to constant abuse by settlers. The international community was alarmed by the rapid deterioration in the city and attempted to broker a new agreement.

In January 1997, the UN made Israel and Palestine sign the Protocol Concerning the Redeployment in Hebron. But the agreement was never ratified. It split Hebron into two areas: H1, a Palestinian area which covered 80% of the city, and H2, the Jewish part. However, there were also Palestinians in H2. The agreement promised to protect these Palestinians with a non-military international force to monitor the situation. The force was only operational for a short while; Israel later forced it to vacate Hebron.

The Palestinians were left defenceless in the face of a concerted campaign of intimidation and harassment that continues to this day. The old city looks like an abandoned war zone.

What was the brand-new Palestinian Authority doing at this time? In theory it had an armed police force at its disposal, but it was never able to intervene effectively. For its own part it was trying to turn itself into a proper government, contemplating elections every now and then, and establishing genuine state institutions. But the disturbances in Hebron and elsewhere revealed its fundamental powerlessness. The PA government was never wholly democratic, and it was no stranger to significant corruption. The future of the Palestinians hence depended on Israel. And it depended on their ability to resist Israel's most brutal policies.

In 1999, Benjamin Netanyahu lost his bid for a second term as prime minister. The Labour Party, under the leadership of Ehud Barak, was back in government.

# 13

# THE SECOND INTIFADA, 2000

When Ehud Barak entered the prime ministerial office, all he wanted was to bring the Oslo Accords to a successful conclusion. He was in luck; the outgoing US president, Bill Clinton, desperately wanted to be remembered for something other than his sexual relations with his intern Monica Lewinsky.

Under pressure from Clinton and Barak, Yasser Arafat was forced to take part in a summer summit in 2000 at Camp David, the US president's country retreat. It was a very strange affair. After seven years of failing to translate the Oslo Accords into actual peace, Clinton and Barak tried to do it in two weeks. They wanted to win some kudos at home. Arafat knew that if he refused to participate, he would be condemned as a warmonger.

At the summit, Arafat tried to navigate around the US and Israeli desire to describe the proposed agreement as a final settlement. He suggested that the agreement would be an interim one, and he would return to Palestine with the good news of fewer checkpoints, fewer settlements and an openness on the Israeli side to negotiate the thornier issues of Jerusalem, the right of return of refugees and a Palestinian state in the future. Barak and Clinton weren't having it. Arafat was asked to call the agreement a final one. That is, he was told to accept no real Palestinian state, no change in the status of Jerusalem and no real solution to the refugee problem. As one of the Palestinian negotiators said in retrospect, 'the biggest distortion is that Barak offered anything.' Arafat refused. As he had anticipated, he was immediately denounced as a warmonger.

Only a few weeks after Arafat returned to Palestine, the leader of the Israeli opposition, Ariel Sharon, paid a provocative visit to Haram al-Sharif, the holy place for Muslims, knowing full well it would incite unrest. Frustrated Palestinians hurled stones at him as he descended from the mount. He then added fuel to the fire by stating, 'The Temple Mount is still in our hands'. The waning hopes of the Oslo Accords ever bringing justice and Sharon's purposeful provocations sparked the Second Intifada.

Unlike the First Intifada, this was a far more militarised uprising, spilling over into Israel itself. Thirteen Palestinian citizens of Israel who protested were shot dead by the Israeli army and police. Islamist resistance groups took up a renewed campaign of suicide bombings within Israel. The deadliest was perpetrated by Hamas: the bombing of Park Hotel in Netanya as Jews celebrated Passover. Thirty died and more than 140 were wounded.

Israel responded with Operation Defensive Shield, in which it effectively reoccupied the West Bank and parts of the Gaza Strip. The operation was much more vicious than the normal regime of collective punishments. Some well-connected Israeli journalists claim this was to compensate for Israel's humiliating withdrawal from Lebanon at the hands of Hezbollah, in the summer of that year.

Israel deployed its air force to bomb cities, massacred people in the Jenin refugee camps and imposed a siege on Arafat in his government's chamber in a compound known as the Mukataa, the former seat of the military governor in Ramallah. They sustained this campaign of repression for years. Only when Arafat fell seriously ill – and there is strong suspicion he was poisoned by the Israelis – and finally passed away in November 2004, did Israel de-escalate somewhat.

Arafat was replaced by Mahmoud Abbas, who was his deputy. Abbas was well aware of the Israeli treatment of his predecessor and took a more cautious approach. He strengthened the Palestinian Authority's co-ordination with the Israeli security services and altogether abandoned armed struggle as a means of resisting the occupation.

Initially this paid dividends. Foreign funding returned for reconstruction projects and for education and welfare, arriving at the PA's ministerial offices or given to local NGOs, provided that they did not contradict the new approach. The PA did permit NGOs critical of its policies to continue work – after all, it wanted to appear respectable to Western eyes. But it was ruthless in targeting political activists, especially those in the ranks of Hamas and Palestinian Islamic Jihad. They not only opposed the PA, but persisted in guerrilla warfare against the occupation.

# 14

## ISRAEL AND PALESTINE IN THE TWENTY-FIRST CENTURY

As the violence subsided, two processes unfolded simultaneously. On the ground, Israel persevered in solidifying its control over all of historical Palestine (the West Bank, the Gaza Strip and Israel itself). Meanwhile the US fruitlessly tried to breathe life into the 'peace process', which had devolved into a bad joke.

### THE MAKING OF THE APARTHEID STATE

In the years following the Second Intifada, Israel intensified the Judaisation of the West Bank and the Jerusalem area. It also further disenfranchised Palestinian citizens of Israel. The Knesset, the Israeli parliament, passed a new wave of legislation, including the infamous Nationality and Entry into Israel Law in 2003. This barred inhabitants of the West Bank and Gaza from being granted automatic citizenship or residency permits through marriage to an Israeli citizen, meaning Palestinian Israeli citizens could find themselves unable to unite with their spouses. This raft of legislation would culminate in the Jewish Nation-State Basic Law in 2018, which downgraded Arabic from a language of the state to one merely protected with 'special status', claimed Jerusalem as the capital of Israel and promoted the expansion of settlements. It gave priority to émigré Jews in terms of citizenship rights.

The road to 2018 was paved with many discriminatory laws. In 2011, the government passed the Nakba law: any official institution that commemorated the Nakba would lose all government funding and protected status. Other laws enshrined the right of Jewish towns and resident areas not to permit the entry of Palestinian citizens of Israel. By the end of the twentieth century, 97% of the land was owned directly or indirectly by Jewish institutions such as the Jewish National Fund (which owns 13% of the land by itself). The Jewish National Fund's charter disallows transactions on land with non-Jews. Many other institutions have similar policies, whether officially or informally. Palestinians, who constitute more than 20% of the population of the state of Israel, are hence generally barred from buying land. So they cannot develop existing towns and villages, let alone build more, while Jewish settlements expand unabated.

In the Naqab, a desert area in the south of Israel, the Bedouins, historically a nomadic population, faced similarly aggressive Judaisation. After the founding of the Israeli state, they were pushed into an area called the Siyag (literally 'fence'), and the 1950 Vegetation Protection Law turned agriculture and grazing, i.e. their primary occupations, into a crime. Throughout the twentieth century, they were forced into towns, and the Israeli government refused to recognise any of their claims to the land. In response, the Bedouins built their own villages without any permission from the state, known as the 'unrecognised villages'. Israel has pursued the demolition of these villages as official policy – most notoriously in the 2011 Prawer Plan, which would have meant the relocation of forty to seventy thousand Bedouins. Bedouins demonstrate remarkable resilience in the face of these challenges: the village of Araqib has been destroyed more than forty times. Each time its residents rebuild it.

Judaisation is hence not merely a policy of gaining territory and building settlements in the West Bank and Jerusalem; it is a policy that stretches over all of Israel. In 2000, Palestinians made up approximately half of the population between the River Jordan and the Mediterranean Sea. Over the decades they have been expelled, ghettoised and purposefully deprived of basic rights. Judaisation requires the perpetual subordination of Palestinians, regardless of where they are in historical Palestine.

While Israel constructed ever more discriminatory legal infrastructure, the West made some pointless gestures towards a peace process – of a sort. The Arab League was willing to negotiate: in 2002 it proposed the Arab Peace Initiative, which would have guaranteed recognition for

Israel across all Arab states and provided for a genuine two-state solution based on the pre-war borders of 1967. In an astounding compromise, the final wording adopted did not mention the right of return for refugees. However, Israel rejected the plan entirely, and the US supported its position.

The baton was passed to a different body altogether: the Quartet, set up as mediators after the failure of the 1991 Madrid Conference. Composed of representatives of the US, the UN, the EU and Russia, it dramatically scaled back its ambitions. It considered Palestinian resistance as the main obstacle to peace, not Israel's expansionism. Unsurprisingly this approach failed to gain much traction. Undeterred, the Quartet tried to offer a new deal: a clampdown under the auspices of the Palestinian Authority on the Palestinian resistance in exchange for freezing Jewish settlements in the occupied territories and an end to the collective punishments imposed upon Palestinians. This failed too.

These attempts intensified after the death of Arafat in November 2004. The new president, Mahmoud Abbas, did not wish to have proper elections, perhaps fearing he would lose his tenuous grip on power. The Palestinian Authority began to lose legitimacy, while Islamist movements gained in popularity owing to their commitment to armed struggle against the occupation.

Hamas in particular performed extremely well in local elections. It was clear that if there were national elections to the Palestinian legislature, it would emerge as one of the largest parties. On the Israeli side, too, politics was becoming more polarised. Since 2001, the scene had been dominated by Ariel Sharon, who had left Likud and subsequently founded an even more extreme party: Kadima.

## ISRAELI DISENGAGEMENT FROM THE GAZA STRIP, 2005

As prime minister, Sharon wanted to break the uneasy impasse. He had a new proposal up his sleeve. To everyone's surprise, in 2003, he proposed removing all the Jewish settlers from the Gaza Strip, roughly eight thousand people, and consequently to relinquish any responsibility for the administration of the Strip. In June 2004, the Israeli government implemented this idea in full – leading to violent clashes on the Strip.

The settlers fought back tooth and nail, unwilling to give up their homes. Ariel Sharon, the man behind multiple massacres, was transformed into an unlikely hero of the peace process. But the withdrawal from Gaza wasn't done for the sake of the Palestinians. It was entirely self-serving. By withdrawing from the Strip, Sharon hoped to 'prove' that Israel couldn't possibly withdraw from the West Bank. It would be too traumatic. The persistent resistance of Hamas had turned the settlers in the Gaza Strip into a liability for Sharon. Gaza, he thought, could become a prison to contain Hamas. And Israel could attack it from the outside, without risking the lives of its own citizens.

By September 2005, the disengagement was complete. Most experts on international law point out that disengagement can't be confused with an end to the occupation. As the new reality on the ground unfolded, it became clear that what Israel was developing was a new model for occupation.

Israel left a power vacuum in the Gaza Strip, and the Palestinian Authority was too slow in filling it. Hamas was in prime position to control the Strip. To try and prevent Hamas from taking over, the Quartet pressured the Palestinian Authority to carry out elections for the parliament of the occupied territories to form a new government. It was obvious that Mahmoud Abbas had no real rivals for the top spot of president.

Elections were held in 2006; Hamas obtained over 44% of the vote. According to the law in the PA, their majority in the Palestinian National Council allowed them to establish a government. And that is exactly what they did, under Ismail Haniyeh, one of their political leaders. However, under pressure from Israel and the US, other parties refused to recognise the government. Israel arrested many of Hamas's members of the Legislative Council and its key activists. Hamas retaliated by abducting an Israeli soldier, Gilad Shalit. He would be held captive for over five years. Realising neither the West nor Israel would accept a Hamas government, Hamas decided to take control of the Gaza Strip by force, through an ugly war against Fatah. This is a black mark in the history of the Palestinian liberation movement. Attempts at unity were made later, but they failed. We need to understand the present evolution of Hamas in this context: when they participated in democratic elections and clearly won, supposedly democratic states simply rejected the outcome. This only prompted further radicalisation. In response, Israel placed the entirety of the Gaza Strip under siege – depriving its inhabitants of many essentials, and frequently limiting their access to water and electricity.

## THE LAST ATTEMPT AT PEACE, 2006–9

While these events unfolded, a new conflict erupted on the Israel–Lebanon border. The Shia militant group Hezbollah abducted three Israeli soldiers it claimed were in Lebanese territory. Israel responded by a second invasion of Lebanon – a new war had started. Israel virtually obliterated south Beirut, bombing thousands of buildings. Hezbollah managed to breach Israel's defences and cause damage with rocket attacks in the north of Israel. After thirty-four days, the war ended once the UN Security Council agreed Resolution 1701. Israel promised to withdraw from south Lebanon, which it had essentially reoccupied, and Hezbollah agreed to withdraw north of the River Litani, so thirty kilometres away from the

Israel–Lebanon border. Neither side upheld their end of the deal. The special UN force appointed to oversee its implementation was powerless to enforce the resolution's terms.

But nonetheless there was some hope for a different future from the end of 2006 to the end of 2008. These were the last two years of Ehud Olmert's government. He had taken over from Sharon after the latter suffered a stroke in 2006.

In a relaxing of previous Israeli intransigence, Olmert was willing to accept the Arab League programme as a basis for negotiations. However, he too was unwilling to give up on the big Jewish settlement blocs in the West Bank, although he offered territorial compensation for them in the Judea desert south of Hebron. This might have had some potential, but there was a big stumbling block. Olmert, like Sharon, and like every other Israeli predecessor no matter how progressive, was unable to countenance a genuinely independent and sovereign Palestinian state existing alongside Israel. Israel wanted a puppet state, one that could never suddenly turn into a hostile neighbour.

But we will never know if something could have come of it, had Olmert persisted. In 2008 he resigned, mired in corruption and bribery allegations, for which he would eventually be imprisoned. His successor was Benjamin Netanyahu, bringing Likud back into power. His pro-gramme was the unilateral expansion of the Judaisation of the West Bank, tightening the siege on the Palestinians in Gaza and solidifying the apartheid regime inside Israel against its Palestinian citizens.

## THE NETANYAHU ERA, 2009–24

When President Obama won the American elections in 2008, there was some hope for another reinvigoration of the peace process. He followed the tried-and-tested American formula for peace-making, regarding the US's role as imposing upon Palestinians the maximum Israel was willing to give. In each iteration, Israel offered less, seemingly to teach the Palestinians a lesson. They wanted to 'punish' the Palestinians for rejecting their 'generosity'. Two rounds of talks under Obama in 2010 and 2012 came to nothing, and the diplomatic stalemate allowed Israel to expand further settlements and continue to oppress the Palestinians. The vigilantes among the settlers in the West Bank became even more belligerent: burning houses, setting fire to fields, uprooting trees and occasionally injuring and even killing Palestinians. The Israeli army did nothing to protect Palestinian civilians.

At the same time Netanyahu's government intensified efforts to Judaise East Jerusalem. With the eager assistance of settler NGOs, funded by right-wing American Jews and Christians, the government began ethnically cleansing neighbourhoods in East Jerusalem such as Sheikh Jarrah and Silwan. This was the new model for Israel's attempt to remove Palestinians from historical Palestine, up until October 2023. Ethnic cleansing would be incremental and small-scale, targeting neighbourhoods rather than whole cities. But it would not stop, not even for a day.

Netanyahu's grip on the government was shaken in the years 2018 to 2020, and multiple snap elections were called. In March 2021, he lost the legislative elections to a very unusual coalition of the main parties, the Islamist Ra'am party and a relatively moderate settlers' party. No wonder it did not survive for very long. During its time in power, in May 2021, for eleven days Palestinians all over historical Palestine united in an attempt to try and end the siege on Gaza, the occupation of the West Bank and apartheid inside Israel. They did not stand a chance. In the ensuing retaliation by Israel, 260 Palestinians were killed.

Netanyahu returned to power in the November 2022 elections. This time he needed the extreme right wing as his partners in the government. Two parties, Otzma Yehudit (Jewish Power) and Ha-Ziyonut Hadait (Religious Zionism), joined the government and held important ministerial positions. The most important was the minister of national security, Itamar Ben-Gvir, and Bezalel Smotrich, the minister of finance. They and other ministers were the graduates of the messianic settlement movement that Judaised the West Bank from 1967 onwards. This movement bred a new generation, to which these ministers belong, of racist and supremacist

Jews, who not only wished to expel the Palestinians from the West Bank but also aimed to impose tighter apartheid on Palestinian citizens in Israel. Ben-Gvir himself was convicted of incitement to racism in 2007. Their ideal for Israel was a theocratic state.

One of the first moves of this new government was an attempt to politicise what was left of the relatively independent Israeli judicial system. It should be noted that the highest judicial authority in Israel, the Supreme Court of Justice, did not stop the colonisation of the West Bank in violation of international law, and consistently upheld the legality of the discriminatory legislation passed against Palestinian citizens of Israel, no matter how often it was appealed.

But for the secular Jews of Israel, it was the last line of defence against the theocratisation of the state. If they were unbothered by the oppression of Palestinians, they certainly were alarmed by the potential repercussions for LGBTQ communities, other minorities and free secular life in cities like Tel Aviv, which, despite the Jewish prohibition on consuming shellfish, has a thriving seafood restaurant scene.

So, when the new government announced the initiation of a legal reform to make the judicial system beholden to the government, secular Israelis took to the streets in their hundreds of thousands to demonstrate against it.

It is revealing that anyone who brought up the issue of the occupied territories in these demonstrations was effectively told to get lost. Secular Israel was not protesting against apartheid Israel, but theocratic Israel.

However, this was a serious challenge not only to the government but to the cohesion of Israeli Jewish society. The leaders of the protest movement belonged to the economic elites of Israel and served as reserves in the special forces and the air force. They threatened to withdraw their capital from Israel and refuse to serve in the army, and some of them started making good on their threats.

When Hamas breached Israeli borders on 7 October 2023, it entered a country on the brink of a civil war. That war was forgotten for the moment, as Israel rallied together to punish every inhabitant of Gaza for the actions of Hamas. But the cracks are only getting wider. There is little common ground between these two camps, which we might call the State of Israel and the State of Judea. The State of Judea is the settler state that grew up in the Jewish settlements in the West Bank. It is now an important political force inside Israel, aiming to turn Israel into a more racist, fascist and theocratic state.

Against them is the State of Israel. This was the old Israel, which prided itself on being the 'only democracy in the Middle East', a secular and pluralist society. That this only held true for its Jewish population did not trouble its conscience too much.

What is clear is that there is no real Left in Israel or even a genuine peace camp anymore. There are of course individuals who still believe sincerely in the possibility of a peaceful solution. And political parties representing the Palestinian citizens of Israel also have a small number of Jewish members. There is a minority who want to work towards justice for all of historical Palestine. But they are marginal, and lack any ability to change the actual policies of the Israeli government.

# 15

## THE HISTORICAL AND MORAL CONTEXT OF 7 OCTOBER 2023

I opened this book with the words of UN secretary general Antonio Guterres, speaking about 7 October 2023. He had made only the mildest reproach of Israel's policies, simply pointing to the reality of a people who have lived for fifty-six years under occupation. If nothing else, I hope you can see the truth in his words. But the reaction in Israel was frenzied.

The Israeli government was quick to condemn the statement. Israeli officials demanded Guterres's resignation, claiming that he supported Hamas and justified the massacre it carried out. The Israeli media also jumped on the bandwagon, asserting among other things that the UN chief 'had demonstrated a stunning degree of moral bankruptcy'.

Israel's reaction to such a senior international figure stating a blatant matter of fact suggests that it is escalating its efforts to censor any questioning of the state and its policies, frequently weaponising the allegation of antisemitism to do so. Until 7 October, Israel invested a great deal of time and energy in building a consensus for a definition of antisemitism that included criticism of the Israeli state and questioning the moral basis of Zionism. Now, even stating that from 1967 generations of Palestinians have grown up under occupation suffices for a witch hunt to be launched against you.

It's useful for Israel for all of us to forget the history, and for any violence on the part of the Palestinians to be seen as a freak atrocity, comprehensible only through the lens of wanting to annihilate Jews. It gives Israel carte blanche to pursue policies it would have shunned in the past, on either ethical grounds or strategic ones. And Western governments follow suit.

The 7 October attack is used by Israel as a pretext to implement genocidal policies in the Gaza Strip. It is also a pretext for the United States to try and reassert its presence in the Middle East. And it is a pretext for some European countries to limit democratic freedoms in the name of a new 'war on terror'. We can see, for instance, how the Berlin police have banned singing and chanting in foreign languages at protests, or how descendants of Holocaust survivors have been arrested at Palestine solidarity demonstrations in the US.

For there to be any hope of peace and justice in Israel–Palestine, we need to remember the key historical context.

We should start at 1948. Most of the people living in Gaza are refugees from the 1948 ethnic cleansing: first, second and now third generation of refugees. Israel created the Gaza Strip as a holding pen so it could ethnically cleanse other areas of historical Palestine. There was no Gaza Strip before 1948. Gaza was a cosmopolitan town on the Via Maris between Egypt and Turkey. This strip of land, only 2% of historical Palestine, became the largest refugee camp in the world.

Since 1967, the inhabitants of Gaza and the West Bank have been under occupation. The people in the West Bank and Gaza are part of the same community, so policies in one area affect the other.

The occupation, whether carried out in the name of the military or a civil administration, made detention without trial, killings, home demolition, expropriation of land and abuse by the army into features of everyday life for Palestinians. In 1987 and 2000, frustration at this ongoing persecution erupted into open resistance: the First and Second Intifadas. It was only a matter of time before a third one broke out. The failure of the two uprisings was also a failure of the more secular Palestinian liberation movement to end the subjugation of Palestinians. Accordingly, many Palestinians found new hope in Islamist groups such as Hamas and Palestinian Islamic Jihad. For them and many Muslims in Palestine, the constant violation of the sanctity of Haram al-Sharif, the Holy Mount in Jerusalem where the al-Aqsa mosque lies, the third holiest place for Islam, was an added insult to the degradation they experienced themselves. Palestinian Christians, one of the oldest Christian communities in the world, had similar grievances regarding how Israel dealt with their holy sites in Jerusalem and Bethlehem. Israel has now destroyed a Greek Orthodox Church in Gaza.

Hamas and other Palestinian groups warned numerous times that continued detention of thousands of political prisoners and the provocations regarding Haram al-Sharif would push them to take drastic action against Israel. They invoked the example of the 2021 movement.

And most recently of all, the Gaza Strip has been subject to an unforgiving siege for seventeen years. Within these seventeen years, Israeli forces have directly attacked Gaza four times, from the land, the sea and the air. Half of the people of Gaza are under twenty-one, so this reality of siege and bombardments is the only one they know. For those of us safe and cosy in our homes, it's hard to grasp the destructive capacity of the bombs that many of our governments sell to Israel. An air bombardment in the twenty-first century is worse than what you have read about in books on the Second World War. Even if you escape injury and death in these bombardments, the trauma will never leave you.

The Hamas fighters who stormed into Israel on 7 October were largely young people who learned the language of violence from the bombs that Israel dropped on them. This is not a justification of what they did. But we should not be so certain that, had we been subject to the same trauma, with no resolution in sight, we would respond much better.

# CONCLUSION

Let me summarise what I hope can be learned from this short book. I have written this book for anyone interested in the history of Israel and Palestine. I hope seeing the injustices inflicted upon Palestinians for over a century now will inspire you to join their struggle in solidarity, and to stand against oppression wherever you are.

First, we have refuted the myth that Palestine was an empty land – a land without a people for a people without a land, as the Zionist slogan goes. It's an utter lie, disproved by any glance at the history books. We've seen what a thriving and diverse society Palestine really was.

No less important is the refutation of the idea that the people who lived two thousand years ago in Roman Palestine were the ancestors of the Zionist settlers who arrived for the first time in 1882. Colonisation cannot be justified based on tenuous connections drawn principally from ancient religious texts. That's not how law or rights work anymore.

The second conclusion is that a Jewish state was built on historical Palestine because it served British imperial interests during and after the First World War. By helping the Zionist movement to build a state (in the period 1918–48), the British violated a promise made to the Palestinians that they would be treated the same as other fledgling nations, i.e. they would be able to exercise a right of self-determination and obtain independence. It also made the British complicit in the eventual 1948 ethnic cleansing of the Palestinians.

The third conclusion is that from the moment the Zionist movement resolved to focus on Palestine as the site of a new Jewish nation, it became a settler-colonial movement. Settler-colonial movements are European settler movements, seeking to build a new Europe outside of Europe where they have been made unwelcome. In all cases, they chose places where other people already live. The native people in those places were viewed by the settler-colonial movements as an obstacle to be removed.

By understanding Zionism as a settler-colonial movement, we can better understand why very early on Zionist thinkers and leaders wrote about the need to transfer the Palestinians. It also explains why even in the mid-1920s the Zionist movement exploited the new land laws of the British to perpetrate the first acts of ethnic cleansing against Palestinian farmers. This ethnic cleansing has continued ever since then right up until today. In 2023, it went to even more violent extremes, costing the lives of tens of thousands of people in the Gaza Strip.

The fourth conclusion is that although many in the West have been willing to extend a hand to other anticolonial struggles, especially when they are against a rival empire, this was never extended to the Palestinians. Through the force of intense pro-Israel lobbying, the Palestinian anticolonialist struggle has been portrayed as brute acts of terrorism, with no good reason behind them. It is time to recognise the Palestinian national movement as an anticolonialist movement. In the global south and among many sections of civil society in the global north, this image of the Palestinian liberation movement as a terrorist organisation is no longer acceptable. But without full global recognition of the Palestinians' right to wage a liberation struggle, the bloodshed in Israel and Palestine will continue.

The fifth conclusion is that the so-called peace efforts were dominated by the USA from 1967, and failed because the US, and its allies in Europe, were dishonest brokers. They always ignored the suffering and the rights of the Palestinians and turned the 'process' into a shield that allowed Israel to continue the occupation and colonisation. In this context, we have shown that the Oslo Accords, hailed as a generous Israeli peace deal that was rejected unreasonably by Palestinians, was nothing of the sort. It was an attempt to substitute one form of occupation with another. It raised hopes that could not be fulfilled and contributed to the outbreak of the Second Intifada.

The sixth conclusion is that the two-state solution, i.e. the main concept informing the so-called peace process, has dismally failed. It has failed because it is not practicable anymore given the presence of 700,000 Jewish settlers in the West Bank and the overall shift of the Israeli political system to the right, which will only be intensified by the events of 7 October 2023. It also can't work because its logical and moral premises are flawed. It applies only to a small part of Palestine (22%) and only to part of the Palestinian people. A genuine solution has to address the problems of the Palestinian refugees and the Palestinian minority inside Israel. This can only be achieved within a one democratic state solution, in which everyone, Palestinian or Israeli, enjoys equal rights and has freedom of movement throughout all of historical Palestine.

The seventh conclusion is that we need to change how we talk about Israel and Palestine. There is no point in talking about peace, as if both sides are equally at fault, when the process we're really talking about is decolonisation. Historical Palestine has been subject to settler colonialism for over a century, at great cost.

Decolonisation is closely associated with other terms that mainstream political discourse in the West avoids when it comes to Israel and Palestine: liberation and reconciliation.

I do not pretend to have a road map as to how these noble aims can be achieved. The Palestinian liberation movement will have to work out how to practically implement a solution – one that offers justice to everyone living in historical Palestine today, including Israeli Jews.

Finally, what we have seen in the Gaza Strip over the last year is the worst chapter in the history of modern Israel and Palestine. In due course, this will be commemorated as an unthinkable catastrophe. It is too soon to predict how it will affect the course of the future and the fate of Palestinians in the years to come. But if we go back to the history, as we've done, we can better understand the connection between the origins of Zionism in Palestine as a settler-colonial movement and its actions that run according to the logic of the elimination of the native. We can understand why we must see the Palestinian resistance as anticolonial first and foremost, notwithstanding the professed ideologies of its participants.

There are other revelations that follow from adopting the paradigm of settler colonialism. It means that any solution in the future will have to take into account that in the last hundred years the Jewish community has grown into a substantial population composed of eight million people. It is a community that has built up a modern state and one of the strongest armies in the world to preserve itself as a Jewish state. And yet it cannot survive, or thinks it can't, without oppressing Palestinians. Palestinians continue to resist, and continue to pose a challenge, despite every attempt at removing them as a community from historical Palestine, ranging from expulsions to brute force and bombings.

It becomes clear that Israel as a Jewish project is not working. There seems to be very little common ground shared by secular and religious Jews in Israel, apart from hatred of the Arabs in general and the Palestinians in particular. That's not enough for a stable national identity – it is not anything that any normal person can persist in taking pride in.

Israeli leaders in our time do not offer any vision for peace and normalcy for Israelis in an Arab world. Israel still sees itself as a Western outpost in a hostile Arab world, even if the majority of Jews in Israel today do not come from Europe. It's only when Israel accepts the reality of its past, and of its closeness to its immediate geographical neighbours, that it can be part of forging a better future for historical Palestine and for the Middle East as a whole. We hope that day comes in our lifetimes.

# FURTHER READING

There is a vast corpus of work by scholars on the Israel–Palestine conflict. This is a short selection of titles covering the events in the book that you might find useful.

Abunimah, Ali. *The Battle for Justice in Palestine* (Haymarket, 2014)

Aked, Hil. *Friends of Israel: The Backlash against Palestine Solidarity* (Verso, 2023)

Allan, Diana. *Voices of the Nakba: A Living History of Palestine* (Pluto Press, 2021)

Erakat, Noura. *Justice for Some: Law and the Question of Palestine* (Stanford University Press, 2020)

Karmi, Ghada. *One State: The Only Democratic Future for Palestine–Israel* (Pluto Press, 2023)

Khalidi, Rashid. *The Iron Cage: The Story of the Palestinian Struggle for Statehood* (Oneworld Publications, 2015)

Khalidi, Rashid. *The Hundred Years' War on Palestine* (Profile, 2020)

Lewis, Geoffrey. *Balfour and Weizmann: The Zionist, the Zealot, and the Emergence of Israel* (Bloomsbury, 2009)

Masalha, Nur. *Expulsion of the Palestinians: The Concept of Transfer in Zionist Political Thought, 1882–1948* (Institute for Palestine Studies, 2012)

Masalha, Nur. *Palestine: A Four Thousand Year History* (I.B. Tauris, 2022)

Mearsheimer, John J., and Stephen M. Walt. *The Israel Lobby and US Foreign Policy* (Penguin, 2008)

Pappe, Ilan. *The Ethnic Cleansing of Palestine* (Oneworld Publications, 2007)

Pappe, Ilan. *The Making of the Arab–Israeli Conflict, 1947–1951* (I.B. Tauris, 2015)

Pappe, Ilan. *Ten Myths About Israel* (Verso, 2017)

Pappe, Ilan. *The Biggest Prison on Earth: A History of the Occupied Territories* (Oneworld Publications, 2019)

Said, Edward. *The Question of Palestine* (Vintage, 1992)

Shambrook, Peter. *Policy of Deceit: Britain and Palestine, 1914–1939* (Oneworld Publications, 2023)

Shlaim, Avi. *The Iron Wall: Israel and the Arab World* (Penguin, 2014)

Shlaim, Avi. *Three Worlds: Memoirs of an Arab-Jew* (Oneworld Publications, 2023)

Shohat, Ella. *On the Arab-Jew, Palestine, and Other Displacements: Selected Writings of Ella Shohat* (Pluto Press, 2017)

Wolfe, Patrick. 'Settler colonialism and the elimination of the native', *Journal of Genocide Research* vol. 8 (2006)

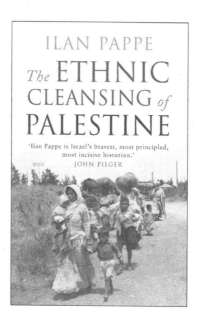

ILAN PAPPE

*The* ETHNIC
CLEANSING *of*
PALESTINE

'Ilan Pappe is Israel's bravest, most principled,
most incisive historian.'
JOHN PILGER

'Along with the late Edward Said, Ilan Pappe
is the most eloquent writer of Palestinian
history.' *New Statesman*

Between 1947 and 1949, over 400 Palestinian
villages were deliberately destroyed, civilians were
massacred and around a million men, women,
and children were expelled from their homes
at gunpoint.

Denied for almost six decades, had it happened
today it could only have been called 'ethnic
cleansing'. Decisively debunking the myth that
the Palestinian population left of their own accord
in the course of this war, Ilan Pappe demonstrates
that, from the very inception of Israel, Zionists sought
to forcibly remove Palestine's indigenous population.

The
Biggest Prison
on Earth
A History *of* Gaza *and the* Occupied Territories
ILAN PAPPE

'Ilan Pappe is Israel's bravest, most principled,
most incisive historian.' *John Pilger*

'Ilan Pappe is Israel's bravest, most principled, most
incisive historian.' John Pilger

In this comprehensive exploration of one of the world's
most prolonged and tragic conflicts, Ilan Pappe analyses
the motivations and strategies of the generals and
politicians – and the decision-making process
itself – that laid the foundation of the occupation in
both Gaza and the West Bank. Ilan Pappe reveals the
legal and bureaucratic infrastructures and brutal security
mechanisms that now incarcerate a population of
nearly five million Palestinians in the world's
largest open-air prison.

**LOBBYING FOR ZIONISM ON BOTH SIDES OF THE ATLANTIC**

ILAN PAPPE

'A magisterial study of the secret weapon of Zionist success in the arena of world politics – the lobby.'
Avi Shlaim

In 1896, a Jewish state was a pipe dream. Today the overwhelming majority of Jews identify as Zionists. How did this happen?

Ilan Pappe unveils how over a century of aggressive lobbying changed the map of the Middle East. Pro-Israel lobbies convinced British and American policymakers to condone Israel's flagrant breaches of international law, grant Israel unprecedented military aid and deny Palestinians rights. *Lobbying for Zionism on Both Sides of the Atlantic* shows us how an unassailable consensus was built – and how it might be dismantled.

ILAN PAPPE is Professor of History at the Institute of Arab and Islamic Studies and Director of the European Centre for Palestine Studies at the University of Exeter. He is the author of over a dozen books, including the bestselling *The Ethnic Cleansing of Palestine*. In 2017, he received the Middle East Monitor's Lifetime Achievement Award at the Palestine Book Awards.